COLONIAL CAPITAL

Colonial Capital

WELLINGTON
1865–1910

Terence Hodgson

RANDOM CENTURY

Random Century New Zealand Ltd
(An imprint of the Random Century Group)

9–11 Rothwell Avenue
Albany, Auckland 10
NEW ZEALAND

Associated companies, branches and representatives
throughout the world.

First published 1990
© 1990 Terence Hodgson
ISBN 1 86941 098 X (cased)
ISBN 1 86941 099 8 (limp)

All rights reserved. No part of this publication may be reproduced or
transmitted in any form or by any means, electronic or mechanical,
including photocopying, recording, storage in any information retrieval
system or otherwise, without the written permission of the publisher.

Designed by Richard King/Edsetera
Printed in Singapore

CONTENTS

Introduction
7

The Beginnings of Commerce
9

Capital City
17

For the Public Good
20

Patterns of Settlement
38

Rich and Poor
41

Illustrations
51

Index
177

INTRODUCTION

To a large extent the title of this book, *Colonial Capital*, describes the limits I have chosen for the work. The word 'colonial' is a time limit, and covers the period up to 1907 when the country graduated from being a colony to being a dominion. The word 'capital' pertains to Wellington as the country's seat of government and provides the other time limit, from 1865. The word 'capital' also focuses the considerations covered in the work to central Wellington. However, these limits are general guidelines. Mention may be made of events taking place before 1865 and after 1907, and of things existing outside central Wellington, particularly in the suburbs and beyond.

Wellington as a European settlement owed its existence to an English-based colonising movement organised by the New Zealand Company. The Company set its sights on a vast portion of central New Zealand and soon convinced itself that it had secured ownership of this land, even though the existing occupiers, the Maori, were not agreed on the terms and conditions of occupation, and were far less aware of the consequences of 'organised' settlement. The New Zealand Company also pursued its claims at the same time that the country was declared a British possession, and the relationship between the Crown and the Company was seasoned with some mutual suspicion.

The New Zealand Company officials and settlers first started arriving in Lambton Harbour in 1839, and made precarious landfall at Petone. This large shelf of sand dunes and swamps was originally considered as the site for the Company's principal city, then referred to as Britannia. However, within months the Company had decided upon the city's present site across the harbour, and named it Wellington after the incumbent Duke back in England.

The city of Wellington was sluggish in growth from 1840 until 1865 and was often viewed sneeringly by other cities. Two earthquakes in 1848 and 1855 greatly reduced citizens' confidence. It was geographically isolated, politically unpersuasive and threatened by the prospect of Maori war parties. Its population growth was slow, with 'arrivals' often only just exceeding 'departures'.

However, once it became the capital, Wellington started to burgeon. The *Evening Post* commented in February 1865: 'Householders, taking advantage of the great dearth of residences of any description, are asking the most exorbitant rents for hovels, lean-tos and shanties of every conceivable build and sort.'

In this book I have sought to trace the city's development as the country's capital, and to look at its major institutions, concerns and social doings through both text and contemporary illustration.

I have looked at Wellington as the seat of government, home of Parliament Buildings, Government House and the vast administrative network associated with a capital city. I have examined its role as a centre of commerce, with its shops, offices, warehouses, factories, banks and bustling waterfront.

Public buildings and amenities are a vital component of a growing city, and colonial Wellington was well endowed with hotels, churches, hospitals and schools, as well as recreation facilities such as libraries and museums, parks and gardens. I have considered their place in the physical and social scheme of the city, and looked also at the development of the suburbs, and the polarisation of rich and poor.

The photographs are gleaned from a number of sources, and extended captions identify the subject and bring in other material that may be immediately relevant.

Contemporary newspapers have provided a lively source of information about colonial Wellington. Their journalistic style adds a certain flavour to events, and varies from damnation to praise, from the explicit to the general, and from the ecstatic to the somewhat coy. Buried in their columns are descriptions of atrocities that today might be found only in forensic reports. Opinions verge on libel, and often a level of editorial sarcasm is employed that would not be acceptable today.

Here, then, is colonial Wellington, warts and all — even if the warts hold most of our attention.

The Beginnings of Commerce

COMMERCE has always been one of the dominant underpinnings of Wellington, embracing everything from single-line traders to large emporia run by entrepreneurs with direct importing facilities. Of course, commerce needed premises, and these contributed much to the changing appearance of the major thoroughfares.

For the first decade of Wellington's settlement, the Te Aro foreshore (a line more or less delineated by present-day Wakefield Street) was the bustling centre of commerce. By the 1850s a new locus of activity had appeared on Lambton Quay, then known simply as The Beach, as its harbour side was still washed by the sea. Lambton Quay until then consisted of small huts, often thatched with raupo. The use of thatch resulted in several fires that destroyed entire blocks of buildings. Raupo was consequently outlawed as a building material by the mid-1840s. The replacement buildings were more solid than the huts. They were largely double-storeyed wooden structures with living quarters for the proprietors upstairs. The shops sold a practical range of merchandise, as was evident by the number of bakers, butchers, clothiers, furnishers, tobacconists, ironmongers, saddlers, and chemists. All their stock arrived by sea, either from other New Zealand ports or Australia and England, and was distributed from bond stores and warehouses. New bulk shipments were advertised widely in the newspapers and caused much excitement among shoppers.

Within a few decades of settlement, and with the increase in population in the new capital, a number of shops dealing in luxuries appeared. Establishments such as piano warehouses, photographers, confectioners, jewellers, toysellers, booksellers, wineshops and hairdressers helped increase the variety of merchandise available. A number of auction rooms, pawnbrokers, public dining rooms and restaurants also began to appear.

In the 1860s the shops of Wellington served a city of only 8,000. The place seemed a rather sleepy hollow to visitors, diarists and tourists. Yet its progress was watched keenly by locals, and monitored by the press, who were eager to report anything new.

It is not surprising that a perceived demand for land in the central city prompted large harbour reclamations. However, building on these new allotments was more sluggish than the City Council (the owner and lessor) might have wished. The reclamation of the harbour side of Lambton Quay gave this street added status as the main commercial thoroughfare, and by the mid-1870s both sides of the Quay were lined with shops, banks and public buildings — some of them of notable architectural merit.

One of the first, and most attractive, blocks of buildings to go up on the new land was a group of three premises designed in 1868 by Danish-born architect Christian Toxward. Delightfully decorated and well proportioned, they helped to usher in a style of architecture that spoke of a certain mercantile confidence and suggested that the practice of architecture could provide a comfortable living.

The 1870s saw a surprising amount of construction in the city centre and a corresponding increase in house building and land subdivision in the inner suburbs of Mt Victoria, Te Aro and Thorndon. Along Lambton Quay and Willis Street numerous new buildings were constructed for both old and recently established businesses. The buildings were almost entirely constructed in wood, which made other cities look down on Wellington and refer to it as a city of 'packing cases' and 'matchboxes'. New hotels, banks, warehouses, churches, schools and government buildings were also going up in relative profusion — signs of confidence and expansion.

Construction in wood was quick and resulted in some charming premises. However, the ravages of weathering and fire dictated a change to construction in brick. Undoubtedly the most dramatic example of brick construction in Wellington was Thomas Turnbull's 1877 design for new premises for Jacob Joseph on Lambton Quay. Joseph, one of the leaders of the small Jewish population of the city, had built his first general store on the site some twenty years before, and continued to build premises for lease almost up until his death in 1903.

Brick construction was more solid and versatile than wood, and was desirable for its better fireproof properties. Wooden construction was gradually outlawed from central city streets from the early 1880s because of the threat of fire. Although the decree was widely adhered to, the government in its determination to cut costs continued to build some of its large projects in wood.

Many fires occurred in the city, but three major blazes stand out for their ferocity, their spread and the number of buildings they annihilated.

In 1879 a fire started in the Imperial Opera House in Manners Street and spread to destroy more than twenty buildings over an area of two hectares, resulting in £50,000 worth of damage. The blaze was so fierce that the red glow of the flames could be seen as far away as Masterton, reflected off the cloud covering over the Rimutaka Hills.

In 1887 a blaze one Sunday morning destroyed six wooden buildings on the corner of Lambton Quay and Panama Street, causing damage to the tune of £100,000. It soon attracted a crowd of about 8,000. The crew of the HMS *Nelson*, in port at the time, offered fire-fighting assistance, and refreshments were provided by a swiftly organised group of ladies. Chemicals stored in Barraud's building and liquor in the vaults of Macdonald's building exploded and made a vivid display of coloured flames. Showers of sparks endangered other buildings in surrounding blocks, and debris and salvaged material clogged the footpaths. The Terrace was lined with spectators who were kept back by a group of sailors with bayonets fixed to their rifles. The fire aroused such interest among Wellington residents that the *Evening Post* produced a

The Beginnings of Commerce

special edition of 9,000 copies, then found they had to run to a second edition.

Perhaps the most alarming central city fire occurred on Lambton Quay early one morning in October 1906. It started in a small wooden building and soon spread to destroy not only a splendid line of new brick buildings adjacent to it, but also all but one building across the Quay on the triangle now occupied by the ANZ tower. Fifteen buildings were destroyed and all the city's fire engines were pressed into service. Halfway through the blaze the main water supply from Wainuiomata stopped, as the pipes burst at Ngauranga. The fire was out by 8.30 a.m. For some distance along the Quay and Willis Street crowds of people were evacuated from hotels, and piles of goods were removed from shops in case more premises went up.

Many of the city's well-known establishments had their beginnings in the early years of settlement, for example the emporia of James Smith (trading as Te Aro House) and Kirkcaldie and Stains, and single-line concerns such as Robert Hannah (footwear), Harcourts and Bethunes (auctioneers and land agents), Gear Meat, and Hallensteins (trading as the New Zealand Clothing Company).

Te Aro House had its beginnings in 1845 as a small millinery business run by two sisters, the Misses Waring-Taylor. In 1868 it was bought by James Smith, who had Thomas Turnbull design new premises. On the upper floor of this new building was a sewing factory turning out fashionable garments. According to an 1883 advertisement, it was 'presided over by one of the most accomplished *modistes* in the Colony.' The building was severely damaged by fire in April 1885, and James Smith quickly engaged Turnbull to design a new brick emporium, which opened in mid-1886. The new Te Aro House proved a success because of its improved appearance and its marketing techniques, which included undercutting prices, cash sales instead of account payments, the continuation of a dressmaking factory on site, vigorous advertising and an extensive mail-order service to country residents.

A city the size of Wellington could only support a limited number of large emporia. Te Aro House's commercial rival was Kirkcaldie and Stains. Both partners of this firm (John Kirkcaldie and Robert Stains) had had drapery experience in England and Australia, and set up in Wellington in 1863.

Five years later the partners bought two lots of reclaimed land and commissioned Christian Toxward to design a new drapery warehouse. This became the nucleus of a large establishment which, after Robert Stains's retirement and return to Scotland in 1891, was run solely by John Kirkcaldie. In 1897 a new richly modelled brick structure designed by Thomas Turnbull went up next to the 1868 shop. Further expansion and the leasing of other buildings for use as showrooms meant the Kirkcaldie and Stains emporium was very well known. It succeeded through low prices, a huge quantity and variety of stock, and a large mail-order service.

During the 1880s a commercial depression hit New Zealand. In Wellington this made itself vividly evident in the number of bankruptcies that were declared or forced, the assigning of estates and merchandise to creditors and a falling-off in building activity. Recovery from the depression was not swift, although it was steady. The beginnings of a new commercial phase started to become apparent in the city in the 1890s. A number of large new buildings were constructed, factories and warehouses were built on the reclaimed land, and shop premises spread into Cuba Street, Manners Street and Courtenay Place. House sites were auctioned in newly subdivided suburbs, and amenities such as libraries, churches, schools and public halls were built. Tunnels and roads were constructed, and pipes for drainage and water supply were laid.

Demand for central city land pushed prices high, which meant taller buildings were erected to regain capital expenditure through rent. At the turn of the century a host of three- and four-storeyed buildings were constructed, with much space available for professional offices. Manufacturers moved their factories to the fringes of the central city or to the new suburbs. This redevelopment produced a streetscape of highly decorated buildings and proved profitable for the leading commercial architects of the time: William Turnbull, William Chatfield, Penty and Blake, and Crichton and McKay. It also spurred on the introduction of new construction techniques, particularly ferro-concrete and the use of steel frames. Credit for pioneering ferro-concrete must go to the large drapery establishment of Veitch and Allan with their four-storeyed block on the corner of Cuba and Vivian Streets, which is still standing, although shorn of much of its decoration. It was designed in 1904 by William Crichton, and the novelty of its construction meant that all tenders received had to be forwarded to the Ferro-Concrete Company in England to be assessed.

The largest private commercial undertaking of this late colonial era was the King's Chambers, built for Macky, Logan and Steen, on the corner of Willis and Willeston Streets. The architect of this towering block of shops and offices was William Chatfield, who produced designs in 1902.

If the city's shops were the 'front door' of commerce, then the warehouses were the 'back door'. Functioning primarily as storerooms for goods, the warehouses were built close to the wharves and by the turn of the century spread along the length of Jervois Quay, Customhouse Quay and Victoria Street to form a veritable barricade between harbour and town.

They were the tall buildings of the city, often decorated on their street frontages but decidedly spartan in their interiors. Great numbers of workers were employed in the warehouses, and the area was a hive of activity. The warehouses were run by magnates, and it was not long before the more prominent ones became household names, and the wealth derived from their enterprises put them in positions of political, social and economic power. Names such as Turnbull, Joseph, Macdonald, Shannon, Nathan, Mills and Johnston were well known in colonial Wellington.

The first group of warehouses were built in wood just off the main shopping streets. Early photographs of Panama and Featherston Streets show how splendidly decorated their facades were. By the 1880s Jervois and Customhouse Quays were becoming the warehouse precincts of the city, spearheaded by the construction of

The Beginnings of Commerce

the W. and G. Turnbull warehouse, designed by Thomas Turnbull (no relation).

Towards the turn of the century it was Victoria Street that took the title of 'warehouse golden mile', especially with the establishment of firms with international backing: Sargood Son and Ewen, Briscoe Macneill, Kaiapoi, and Bing Harris. Victoria Street reached its zenith in the first decade of the new century with the construction of the towering Hayman warehouse designed in 1905 by William Chatfield. Chatfield had been practising in the city since 1875, and was responsible for the design of many of Victoria Street's buildings. Such was the intricacy of department and sample rooms in the Hayman warehouse that it was necessary to have an internal telephone exchange installed, a pioneering form of the now-common PABX.

These large warehouses were merchandise treasure troves, and the quantity of goods available meant that individual floors were given over to single lines. General merchants like W. and G. Turnbull, and Hayman, owned their own ships to import goods from overseas. There were also specialist merchants dealing in a limited number of goods. For example, H. C. Gibbons's seed warehouse on Lambton Quay (next to Jacob Joseph's building) had entire floors set apart for gardening tools, English grass seeds, local grass seeds and manure.

MANUFACTURING was closely related to warehousing, yet Wellington did not attain the scale and importance in this area that other cities did. However, several Wellington-based concerns did well for both their shareholders and the city. One of these was the Gear Meat Company, which had its beginnings as a butcher's shop on The Beach. In 1870 they had new premises built, and three years later they embarked on preserving and canning meat for local and export consumption. The business was so successful that the factory was relocated to the new industrial area of Petone and for decades added all manner of new products and ancillary buildings to their works.

More numerous than the large firms with export drives were the local manufacturers of such items as clothes, jewellery, saddlery, confectionery, furniture, bricks and aerated water. Small workshops employing a handful of people made up the broad base of industry for the city, yet only a few businesses expanded to the point where they became public companies with branches in other cities. Local industry sometimes took the form of something specific and seemingly trivial, such as Bryant and May's match factory; or it was labour-intensive and aimed at a small market, like Rouse and Hurrell's coach-building factory; or it was service-oriented, like the numerous steam laundries that sprang up in the 1880s. However, while local industry was welcomed for its obvious contribution to the economy, it was also exposed in the press and official circles for its fearfully low wages, overcrowding, poor ventilation, long working hours and less than reasonable safety standards. Improvements in conditions were sought in a variety of ways, including a raft of labour legislation, committees of inquiry, public campaigns and the effective action of individuals. Perhaps the most vigorous campaigner in this respect was Samuel Parnell, who, from his cottage in Alpha Street, instituted the widely celebrated eight-hour working day.

Colonial Capital

BANKING was one of the first public services to be established in fledgling Wellington. The Australian-based Union Bank, which later contributed to the formation of the present ANZ group, was the first to open its doors. It built premises in 1852 on the corner of Willis and Boulcott Streets — a single-storeyed banking chamber with a spacious manager's house built at right angles to it. The building was superseded by new premises at the apex of Lambton Quay and Featherston Street in 1874. Designed by Christian Toxward, this building was a splendid example of wooden craftsmanship, with generous, Greek-inspired detailing. It burnt down in 1906 and was replaced by a much larger building. The position of the site assured the Union Bank considerable visual prominence.

Further along the Quay and also on an apex site (formed by Customhouse Quay), was the Bank of New Zealand's Wellington office. The BNZ was established by a group of Aucklanders as a local alternative to the numerous overseas-owned banks trading in New Zealand. They secured their Wellington site shortly after the bank's formation. Plans for a building were drawn up by Mason and Ross of Dunedin in 1863. Within a few years of completion the building was found inadequate, and Thomas Turnbull was called in to enlarge it in 1877. This building was sold for removal in 1898, and work began on one of the city's most imposing and best-loved structures, the BNZ head office, also the work of Thomas Turnbull. He was given the job after winning the bank's design competition, which was organised for a different site. Turnbull's plans sported three grand towers at the corners of the building. However, these were dispensed with in the sort of budgeting exercise that has typified so many of the country's more ambitious building schemes.

INSURANCE has always been a close relative of banking. The establishment of insurance companies in colonial Wellington was as steady and as inevitable as the establishment of the banks. One of the most obvious fields for insurance was fire, the scourge of any wooden settlement. In the fledgling days of fire insurance the companies issued plates to be fixed to the clients' buildings so that in event of fire, the relevant insurance company could identify the building as one of their own and proceed to fight the fire. It may seem an odd procedure, but it stems from the fact that insurance companies often owned the only effective fire engines.

Fire had a propensity to spread, and was no respecter of insurance company policy. It was not until the establishment of volunteer fire brigades in the city in the early 1870s that insurance companies could develop their policies and pay-outs rather than their fire engines. While levies were high in wooden Wellington and buildings were often under-insured, the prudence of insurance was seldom doubted.

The threat of arson was also a good reason to take out fire insurance. In the 1880s the incidence of arson attacks was particularly disturbing. The Chamber of Commerce, noting that the local insurance companies paid out nearly sixty percent of their reserves in claims in 1887, called for flogging and long prison terms for arsonists.

Marine insurance was also important at the time. It was available either from the large companies that had a

The Beginnings of Commerce

separate marine department or from small companies dealing solely in this line.

The premises of the insurance companies operating in colonial Wellington followed a building pattern similar to that of the city's shops and banks — decorated wooden buildings in the 1870s, progressing to tall brick structures around the turn of the century. As they were built in the central city, it is not surprising that none are still extant.

WATERFRONT and harbour works were an integral part of colonial Wellington. The city's main gate was the waterfront and by it came the bulk of imports: clothes, food, hardware and building materials. It was the main method of transport to other parts of the country and overseas. It also provided a natural setting for recreation.

As the European settlement of Wellington progressed, numerous jetties and wharves were built for loading and unloading vessels. Many were 'private', that is, they were built by local merchants and were known by their builders' names: Pearce's Wharf, Plimmer's Wharf, Levin's Wharf, Rhodes's Wharf, etc. Some were very flimsy and prone to collapse in heavy swells; others were sturdy and long enough to reach deep water at low tide, which suited the larger vessels.

Holding pride of place in the annals of early social history was 'Noah's Ark', the wreck of the *Inconstant*, which hit rocks at the harbour heads in 1849. John Plimmer had it brought to a site off Lambton Quay, now the site of the 'old' BNZ building. He stabilised it by packing it in and built warehouse space on top of it.

Despite the proliferation of private wharves, there was a need for a large, deepwater public wharf. In 1862 the Provincial Council funded the construction of Queen's Wharf, which was about 170 metres long and cost £15,500 to build. It subsequently underwent several expansions and improvements. For some decades this was the city's major wharf and it was often congested. In February 1874 the *New Zealand Mail* called the wharf an 'al fresco storehouse with its stacks of wool bales, piles of timber, heaps of railway iron, packages of merchandise, tanks of malt, parts of locomotives and carriages, barrels of cement, cases of kerosene, and articles of coastal commerce.' The wharf also provided a sleeping place for many of the city's homeless. In February 1876 the *New Zealand Mail* observed a few people even had blankets and pillows, 'the which style of sleeping, being most civilised, is most scarce.'

Flat land was required by commerce, industry, the government and the railways. As a result large-scale harbour reclamations were undertaken, which vastly altered the original line of the foreshore. Some of the first reclamations were carried out by private concerns and were only large enough for the building constructed on it. This was the case with the two masonic hall sites on Lambton Quay.

The first major reclamation of about five hectares was started in 1866, and effectively pushed the harbour several blocks away from Lambton Quay. The second major reclamation was started in 1874 and reached from Thorndon to Hunter Street. The contract for this work was let to Saunders and O'Malley for close to £56,000. It was paid for by the Provincial Council, who sold it to the Wellington City Council on completion in 1878 for

£89,000. These prices may seem high, but it worked out that the City Council paid only £10 per foot when some central city land was already selling at £150 per foot. The 1874 reclamation covered almost nineteen hectares and was the largest such infill. Before work could begin a vast order for jarrah had to be placed in Australia to form the breastwork behind which the spoil was dumped. Pile driving was done by steam engines moored on punts, while the spoil came from quarries along the Kaiwharawhara Hills and was transported to the reclamations by rail.

Blasting and quarrying were undertaken by gangs of men working four-hour shifts, who were sometimes secured by ropes high up on the cliff faces. Falls and slips were common, and injuries and deaths sometimes occurred. Accidents prompted public inquiry, and after one man had his leg squashed, the *Evening Post* reported, 'it is to be regretted that there is no accident fund in connection with the work' (July 1876). The press kept its readers informed of the new appearance of the city as work progressed, and seemed happy that the old shoreline was being obliterated: '. . . in all probability next week will see the foul and polluted foreshore, which so long has disgraced Lambton Quay, shut out forever,' declared the *Evening Post* in March 1877.

The Thorndon and Lambton Quay reclamations progressed relatively smoothly. By contrast, the two reclamations of the Te Aro area, which contributed a further sixteen hectares of land, were dogged by problems. Foreshore owners pressed for compensation for the loss of their sea frontage — Bethune and Hunter put in a claim for £10,000 even as late as 1884. There were disagreements about the line for the reclamation limit. Bankruptcies and heavy swells also created problems, as did the arguments about where to take the spoil from. In 1882 the contractor Peter McGrath undertook to complete twenty-three acres (about nine hectares) of the Te Aro scheme, but two years later he went bankrupt and a battle began over the assets. McGrath had constructed a splendid trestle railway, which brought spoil from Oriental Bay to the site in trucks drawn by a little steam engine called *Pio Pio*. The decision to use spoil from Oriental Bay was made after the other suggested quarry, Polhill Gully, was turned down because of the inconvenience it would cause to hundreds of Te Aro residents. In 1884 the City Council sought and received permission to raise a loan of £75,000 to complete the work; and by 1885 progress was again underway. By 1889 the many stages of the Te Aro reclamation were finished, the spoil for the final section coming from the Wadestown hills.

Capital City

WELLINGTON was elevated to position of capital of the colony in 1865 mainly because of its geographical centrality. The decision reflected the recommendations of a committee appointed to look into the matter, and was supported by South Island Members of Parliament. The move from Auckland meant accommodation had to be provided for the Parliament, the Governor, civil servants and various departments, giving rise to a variety of interesting buildings.

Parliament's first home in Wellington was a Gothic-style building originally constructed for the Provincial Council in 1857. Its architect, George Single, had foreseen that Wellington would become the capital, and had two large debating chambers incorporated into his design, one for the lower house (the House of Representatives) and the other for the upper house (the Legislative Council). Although additions and improvements were made to Single's structure, by the early 1870s a much larger building was required. The Colonial Architect William Clayton designed the new Parliament Buildings built in Sydney Street. The design took its stylistic cue from Single's small Provincial Council building. The Gothic style was used with great vigour, and the building became an impressive addition to the city's architecture until its destruction by fire in 1907.

Demands for the satisfactory housing of the General Assembly's vast library had been made almost since the collection was started. In 1898 work eventually began on a special library building — a florid brick and plaster structure built on the site of Single's first government building of 1857. The new General Assembly Library was designed by Thomas Turnbull but reduced in height by the Public Works Department — a move that made Turnbull demand his name be removed from the marble foundation stone, which was done by simply covering it up with cement. Part of a newly built wall had to be pulled down to install the stone, and the ceremony went ahead with little public notice.

Another important building of central government was the house for the colony's Governor. On arriving in Wellington the Governor had to make do with a house originally built for Colonel Wakefield, the nucleus of which had been brought out from England in prefabricated sections. In 1865 this Government House was extended with a new wing that did not appeal much to the press. The *Evening Post* thought it 'not unlike the stuccoed bay windows and green verandahed edifices so much in demand at second-rate watering places in the old country' (August 1865). Three years later a large ballroom was built at the back of Government House in preparation for the visit of Prince Alfred to the colony in 1869. The ballroom was considered such a makeshift barn that it was commonly referred to as the 'shedifice'. It was demolished before the Prince arrived. In 1868 the government looked for suitable sites for a new Government House. It finally decided that the existing site was adequate, although a new building was obviously needed. The old building was destined to end up as a soap factory in Murphy Street. The new Government House was designed by William Clayton, who was living in Dunedin at the time, which caused much grumbling. 'We do not know why this course has been taken; there are surely architects in this city of equal merit,' suggested the *Evening Post* in November 1868.

Completed in 1871, this Italianate building was demolished in the late 1960s to make way for the Beehive. Its function as Government House had been superseded back in 1910 with the completion of the present Government House in Newtown.

WITH the housing needs of the Governor and Members of Parliament catered for, it was now the turn of the civil service. They were housed for a short time under one roof in a building designed by William Clayton in 1873. On calling tenders, Clayton was shocked both at the high prices for the wood needed and the wages of the carpenters. New tenders were sought for the design in both wood and concrete, as well as tenders for the two and a half acres (one hectare) of land which needed to be reclaimed for the building to proceed. The first building tenders were declined, but Clayton persevered until a local firm, Archibald and Scoullar, offered to build the project for about £30,000, with the government supplying the timber and the paint. By mid-1876 the north wing was complete and the Treasury moved in with little public ceremony; the rest of the building was occupied by the end of the year.

Clayton's Government Building remains today one of the city's and the country's favourite buildings of the colonial era.

Although central government had moved to Wellington in 1865, provincial government was not disbanded for another ten years, and the Provincial Council had to have new premises after their building was taken over by Parliament. The new Provincial Council Building, yet another wooden structure, was designed in 1871 by Christian Toxward for a site on Customhouse Quay and was built for £8,000.

The City Council (then called the City Corporation) also needed a building to work from. Like a third tier of civil administration, the Council handled all manner of business from roadworks to dog licences and setting tariffs for hansom cabs. In 1877 Thomas Turnbull designed a grand formal building for the City Council in Featherston Street, which served them until the Council's move to the new Town Hall in 1905.

Not surprisingly, the expanding civil service soon found their wooden building of 1875 was too small for all their departments, and the years around the turn of the century saw some large buildings go up to house the Government Life Insurance and the Public Trust Office.

The Government Life had its first home in the 1872 Provincial Council Building on Customhouse Quay, and in 1893 it had a new and rather interesting building designed for the same site by Clere, FitzGerald and Richmond.

The Public Trust also had its first offices in the Provincial Council Building. In 1905 it finally moved into its new building on Lambton Quay, designed by John Campbell, the Government Architect.

Throughout the country, post offices were prominent government buildings. However, Wellington had to wait decades before it got a building worthy of the city's status as the capital. Its first post office of any note was built in 1862 and looked more like a shed with a time ball on the roof. However, this building on Customhouse Quay was to claim the entire block for post office use. Calls for a new post office had been made long before the large brick building appeared in 1882. The Colonial Architect Pierre Burrows had drawn up designs for a three-storeyed building in 1879, but it never got off the drawing board. Later in 1879, new designs were invited and a pamphlet was issued outlining all the requirements, apart from the style. However, entries were refused because the Postmaster General thought they would far exceed the £17,000 budget. Two years of indecision lapsed before Thomas Turnbull was given the job on 'fast track' in 1881. A tender price of almost £23,000 was accepted from builders Barry and McDowell.

The General Post Office was badly damaged by fire in 1887, after which the building was fully reinstated.

For the Public Good

BUILDINGS and amenities for public use provide a glimpse into one of the most contentious areas of the city fabric. Anything backed by public money was open to criticism, not just for its appearance, but also for its running, its cost and its benefits or lack thereof. However, any sizeable town demands amenities like schools, libraries, parks, hospitals, transport and drainage, and it was the town's elected councils who had to provide them by juggling budgets, raising loans and undertaking the unenviable task of according them priority.

The private sector also provided buildings and amenities for public use, although the possibility of economic failure was apt to abort them in the planning stages. Any city has a shelf, or a rubbish tin, full of ventures that never got off the ground. Two such abandoned proposals for colonial Wellington were an Anglican cathedral on Taranaki Street, and a Catholic cathedral on Buckle Street.

HOTELS have always been among the first public buildings to make an appearance in early settlement, and Wellington could boast a fair handful of them within months of being established on Lambton Harbour. Many of them were little more than grog shops, but there were those offering accommodation, meals, and also space for public assembly.

After Wellington became the capital, the hotels burgeoned in all respects: in size, number, architectural flair, interior appointments and tariffs. They were privately owned, either by individuals or syndicates, and frequently underwent changes of ownership, name or physical appearance. They were the larger, more imposing buildings on the streets, and were required by law to burn lamps above their front doors during the night. For the greater part they offered both accommodation and bars. The accommodation could either be single rooms or grand suites, could be rented out long-term or even permanently. Staying guests came from many different walks of life: tourists (both local and overseas); people on transfer (especially civil servants); and visiting entertainers and country residents coming into town.

In addition to a variety of bars, the better hotels also offered dining rooms and specific areas like 'commercial rooms', smoking rooms, billiard rooms and ladies' lounges. Some had what were known as 'blood rooms' — rooms where bodies were removed to when found at night and where coroner's courts might sit. This sombre function disappeared when a morgue was built, but it was roundly found distasteful. The *Evening Post* (September

1871), on hearing that the three-week-dead body of a drowned man had been taken to a blood room, declared that it was scarcely 'in a state in which any private individuals would have liked to receive it into their houses'. Each time a body was removed to a hotel for an inquest, the publican received a fee of one pound for the inconvenience.

The hotels were big employers, especially of women, but they were also fire traps. Luckily, few deaths occurred as a result of fire, but many premises were lost. Notable hotels razed by fire include the Melbourne (Willis Street, 1901), Orr's City Buffet (Lambton Quay, 1888) and the Royal Oak (Cuba Street, 1898).

Around the turn of the century a number of new brick hotels went up in Wellington — a move paralleled in most other major cities. They may have been the last word in comfort, appointments and fire safety, but in appearance most were extremely ungainly looking.

Somewhat different in function, churches also began to appear in the early days of colonial Wellington. The dominant denomination was Anglican, with large numbers of Catholics, Presbyterians and Wesleyans. Although Congregationalists, Baptists, Salvationists and Jews were in the minority, they still built their own places of worship. In the early days there were also brief sightings of Mormons (a group of them set up a camp in Karori in the 1870s), and Spiritualists (who held sporadic lectures in the Te Aro area in the 1880s). Judging by the fund-raising activities, bequests in wills, gifts, and the subscription lists and pledges, the church as a building was probably more meaningful to colonists than to us today. The first pioneer churches were adequate for a time, yet by the 1860s most established congregations aspired to buildings of some presence. Among the first impressively well-designed, though not necessarily large, churches were: St Paul's in Mulgrave Street (1866); St Mary's in Hill Street (1866); the Jewish Synagogue on the Terrace (1869); St Peter's in Willis Street (1878); St Mark's at the Basin Reserve (1876); St John's in Willis Street (1884); and St Andrew's on the Terrace (1878).

These churches were designed by architects who were trained in the Gothic style, but did not always have a thorough understanding of the abilities of wooden construction. One frequently encountered problem was the fierce local wind, which could rock a church dramatically. Buttresses were sometimes built to stabilise the church, or parallel aisles and transepts were added. The demand for increased seating also gave rise to some architectural innovation. Many of the city's early churches were added to several times, often involving some delicate dismantling and refitting. St Paul's in Mulgrave Street is the most striking example. As the *Evening Post* reported in February 1876, 'it always seems to be in a chronic state of alteration and enlargement.'

A number of the city's well-known wooden churches have been lost to fire.

The first to go was the Manners Street Methodist Church in 1879. The Methodists did not rebuild on the site. Instead they moved to the splendid classically styled St John's Church on the corner of Willis Street and Macdonald Crescent, which had been built in 1876 to designs by Thomas Turnbull. Five years later this church went up in flames and was replaced by the present St John's, also designed by Thomas Turnbull.

In 1898 fire destroyed the well-known St Mary's Catholic Church in Hill Street. The fire was started by painters using charcoal burners to strip old paint from the tower. It occurred early in the morning, but still managed to attract a vast number of bystanders. Its replacement is the present basilica, designed by Dunedin-based architect Francis Petre, whose work for the Catholic Church was both prolific and grand.

In 1918, fires badly damaged both St Andrew's Presbyterian Church on the Terrace and St Mary's Catholic Church on Boulcott Street. The replacements for both churches were designed by Frederick Clere using the relatively new construction method of reinforced concrete. Both buildings are still standing, and both are acknowledged as landmarks of their respective streets.

THE machinery of justice was quickly established in Wellington. Its first buildings were as rudimentary as any other place of official work, and it was not until 1863 that the city got its first decent-looking Supreme Court building. The site was Lambton Quay and the structure was designed and built by Charles Carter, a well-known contractor who was later involved with small-farm settlement in the Wairarapa and after whom the town of Carterton was named. A sturdy building with a severe and formal facade, the Supreme Court only served judicial needs for eighteen years. In 1881 a new Supreme Court was opened nearby on newly reclaimed Stout Street.

This building was the work of Pierre Burrows, who had taken over the position of Government Architect after William Clayton's death in 1877. Burrows produced a design that drew on the style of Greek temples, with plenty of decoration and an upper floor set back from the line of the ground floor.

Excavations were required to the original bedrock four metres below street level, but about two-thirds down, the rush of water into the hole was such that pumps had to be used continuously. Bystanders shook their heads and said the contractors 'might as well try to pump the harbour dry' (*New Zealand Mail*, April 1879). Undeterred, the contractors set the concrete foundations underwater in iron casings and construction went ahead.

In December 1879 all was ready for the foundation stone laying ceremony. It attracted hundreds of spectators and a special platform was built for the convenience of ticket-holding ladies. A grand Masonic procession with a guard of honour provided by the New Zealand Artillery, City Rifles and the Naval Brigade made a splendid display, as did the ceremony of pouring vases of corn, oil and wine over the foundation stone — and all this punctuated by several hymns sung to the accompaniment of a borrowed cabinet organ.

Court hearings were regularly written up in the press, often providing details of the prisoner's appearance, habits and clothes, as well as the process of cross-examination. For example, the *New Zealand Mail* (May 1880) provided this description of two people who had been apprehended in an unoccupied house in Boulcott Street and charged with vagrancy: '[the man had] a quantity of red stubble about his chin, and a green patch over the right eye . . . his companion . . . as if to compensate for the absence of a green patch over her eye, held a corner of her shawl to that organ, and thus effectively eclipsed the dexter side of her physiognomy.' They were sentenced to fourteen days hard labour.

For much of the time the charge sheets were full of petty crime. During the 1880s hearings of vagrancy and small thefts were common — a mark of tough economic times.

If such crime provided the public with interesting reading, the hearing of serious charges provided them with extraordinary reading and topics for conversation. The charges included the occasional murder, infanticide, the running of brothels, and attempted suicide. Public interest was also stirred by the gambling and opium-smoking charges drawn from the Chinese quarter of the city.

Punishment was usually a fine or imprisonment — and imprisonment was often the alternative to the inability to pay fines. Incarceration was at the local prison and was a regularly meted punishment, even for minor offences. Vagrancy could easily attract a few weeks' stay with hard labour, and theft of clothes or a few pounds could earn up to a year in jail, also with hard labour. Serious convictions were punished by flogging, carried out under medical supervision and in the presence of the press. In February 1877 the *Evening Post* carried a full description of two men sentenced to fifty lashes each (done in two 'shifts') for rape. The correspondent described both the triangle to which the men were strapped, the 'cat' (a whip that had nine one-metre long cords with knots tied in them) and the results of the flogging. 'At the fifteenth stroke his back was severely marked, and by the time the full quantum of twenty-five lashes had been administered, the right shoulder was much cut, and bits of the flesh or cuticle had been picked out by the knots in the "cat",' observed the writer.

The Wellington jail was situated high above the city on what is now the south end of the Terrace. Although it was called the Terrace Jail, for most of its existence that part of the Terrace was called Woolcombe Street. The jail was established along with the city. Overcrowding and miserable conditions seemed to dog it from the outset. Within a year of Wellington becoming the capital the *Evening Post* lamented the prison was so full of criminals it would be necessary to build a new wing. The hard labour and convict wards were already full and there seemed to be 'no lack of debtors and females in the other quarters.'

When votes of money came through, the Terrace Jail was added to and soon became a warren of various buildings in a park-like setting of three hectares. By the 1880s the complex almost required a map to make sense of the layout. There was a debtors' room with its own exercise yard, a long-sentence block with single cells sometimes sleeping up to four people, punishment cells in total darkness with double doors, solitary confinement cells half underground, a hospital ward, a boys' prison with its own separate living room, remand wards, cells for drunks, a hard labour ward and a female ward.

Within the high walls of the prison, and under the

vigilance of armed guards, a daily routine was established. The prisoners rose at 5.30 a.m. and after breakfast of tea and bread, the hard labour gangs left for work at 7.00 a.m. They worked until 5.00 p.m., with a lunch break of yet more tea and bread. After a dinner of boiled meat, the prisoners devoted a few hours to education when they might learn to read and write. Then they were locked up for the night at 8.00 p.m. Sundays were free of work, and along with compulsory divine service and a compulsory bath, there was a library which had a fair selection of magazines and, according to the *Evening Post* of April 1881, plenty of novels with a 'preponderance of the "goody goody" element.'

In 1881 the government granted money for the building of a huge prison on a plateau of land overlooking the Te Aro flat. This was the site of the Mt Cook Barracks and had been used variously as an immigration depot, a jail for Maori prisoners, and barracking for local militia volunteers. The government's aim was to provide a prison for the central region of the country — a major prison like Auckland's Mt Eden and Christchurch's Lyttelton Jail. The scheme provoked unease among the citizens, and protests about putting such an institution in a city on such a commanding site were quickly raised. No notice was taken of the protests, yet they continued forcefully while the building was being constructed.

The fortress was never used as a prison, and in 1903 it was officially designated the Alexandra Military Barracks. This decision also drew protest from those who thought a central city barracks would lower the status of the surrounding neighbourhood. Moves had also been made to use the building as the city's university. (The university had no permanent home until the opening of its Kelburn Parade building in 1906.) The Mt Cook Jail had also been deemed a suitable building for the country's parliament, a mildly humorous suggestion made by the Hon. William Larnach in 1897, who went on to suggest the present House of Parliament would itself make a good university.

Designed by the Government Architect Pierre Burrows, the Mt Cook Jail was a fearsome piece of work with a floor plan of wings (not all built) radiating from a central guard tower, walls of thick brick, single cells lined up like cages and basement accommodation for kitchens, laundry, workshops and punishment cells.

It was built by prisoners, who made the bricks and reduced the three and a half hectare site by about five metres. The brickmaking yard was an industry in itself, and supplied millions of bricks for both the prison and other buildings in the city. A prisoner could turn out 2,000 bricks a day on average, and the area soon became a vast factory with huge numbers of drying sheds, a massive firing kiln and tramways for trucks pulled either by horses or the prisoners themselves. Several contingents of prisoners were brought from Napier and Lyttelton to help with the work.

Work proceeded apace and it seemed nothing could stop it, not even the Wellington City Council, who offered to buy the area from the government in 1886. The Council's offer of £5,000 fell well short of the £20,000 already spent on the project by the government and, besides, it was deemed the prisoners were better kept busy than idle.

For the Public Good

By 1897, one wing was ready for occupation but the jail was destined never to be used for penal purposes.

WELLINGTON was just as short of medical funds and adequate health facilities as any other colonial settlement. During the period of provincial government it had to vie for funds with every other public sector. This continued as a feature under central government until the establishment of controlling boards. To a large extent ill-health was viewed as a misfortune, and primary health care was seen as the responsibility of doctors and the patients' families. The public hospital, as a building and an institution, was more a charitable organisation. Its patients were mainly drawn from the poor, who could not afford private treatment or hadn't the means to be nursed at home.

In 1847 a hospital had opened its doors in Pipitea Street, functioning mainly as a centre for major surgical cases and Maori health. It was severely damaged in the 1848 earthquake and a replacement was built in 1852 to house forty patients. This colonial hospital (see page 113) may have looked pleasant enough, but inadequate funding from the Provincial Council, lack of structural maintenance, overcrowding and a reticence from people to pay for their treatment soon made it a place to be avoided if possible.

Many of the patients were simply old and decrepit 'such as in England would be in the poor-house' (*Evening Post*, March 1878). Overcrowding was common: wards intended for a maximum of thirty were found to be sleeping over fifty. Rules were laid down for such things as outpatient advice and vaccination times. Visiting hours were restricted to six hours a week, which the hospital authorities reminded the public were 'far more extended than those in force at the London hospitals.'

The hospital's use as a dumping ground for the poor came graphically to light after one of the patients, arrested for stealing flowers off graves, was found to have lived at the Thorndon hospital for the past twelve years.

In 1875 Christian Toxward drew up new hospital plans for a site in Newtown. This large site offered good sun and drainage after the necessary earthworks were carried out. Toxward's plan for a building of radiating wings in a garden setting was in line with overseas developments in healthcare architecture. However, work on the project was extremely slow. Construction did not begin until 1878, and patients did not move in until the winter of 1881.

Prison labour was used to produce the bricks required. They cost £1 per thousand, which was a third the cost of buying them elsewhere in the country. The good quality clay of the area made brickmaking worthwhile, and although Toxward's quantity survey called for two million bricks, the output of about 40,000 a week was deemed satisfactory. The prisoners were also responsible for levelling and laying out the grounds in lawns and trees.

Brick construction was relatively new for Wellington, and when it came to plastering the building, it was hard to find plasterers: '. . . artisans are reluctant to come from Australia just for one job' (*New Zealand Mail*, December 1878).

After the hospital was completed, the brickmaking

works, the special moulding machinery (imported from America) and a huge quantity of bricks were put up for auction. Toxward himself secured 200,000 bricks as he intended building a large house in nearby Wright Street.

In any colonial settlement one major area of medical attention was the treatment of accident and injury. With so much physical labour, severe injury was common. People often lost limbs or were crushed while working on projects such as roadmaking, reclamation or construction, and in iron foundries, factories and warehouses or while operating transport.

However, infectious diseases were also a source of medical concern. Outbreaks of epidemics like typhoid, scarlet fever, dysentery and diphtheria were common. These diseases thrived and bred in areas of stagnant water, high rat populations, and with no drainage apart from cess-pools dug outside back doors. These areas were the city slums, where the overcrowding of both people and buildings exceeded even the limits set down by the councils of European cities.

Wellington's slums were not huge in area, but *per capita* they were not to be ignored. Neither was the infant mortality rate, which at its worst could rise to a staggering eighty percent. It seemed every year the city was visited by plague, and the blame was laid on everything from drainage to the condition of the cemetery, from pigsties within city limits to night-soil depots. In the late 1870s the water supply at Polhill Gully contained so many dead animals that it was deemed to be twice as impure as the worst water supply in London. In February 1876 the *Evening Post* wrote: 'We can hardly believe that there is any other city in the world where the inhabitants are allowed to drain all their filth into open gutters . . . it is not surprising to hear that the usual summer epidemics are setting in with great virulence . . . Three funerals passed along the beach in one day last week, and the death-roll is springing up with terrible strides.'

Even as late as the 1890s typhoid killed many people and the hospital could barely cope. One particular outbreak in 1892 even made news in Australian, English and American newspapers, although it was undoubtedly overdramatised. Typhoid was also suggested as the reason why the Governor, Lord Onslow, resigned and a replacement was hard to find. When the City Council asked ratepayers in late 1892 to sanction a £165,000 loan for a drainage scheme, it was not surprisingly upheld by an overwhelming majority.

Perhaps the most fearful time in respect of public health was the bubonic plague scare of 1899. The plague had reached Australia, and the bacteria were found in New Zealand but not in Wellington, where extreme precautions were taken and thoroughly implemented.

Shipping in Wellington harbour was controlled with ruthless severity. All incoming ships were required to moor away from the wharves at night to reduce the possibility of rats coming ashore, all their ropes had to be kept tarred and sticky, gangways had to be kept up, floodlights were erected on the wharves, night watches were introduced and no ship was allowed to discharge into the harbour.

On land, all buildings in the city were inspected by the Health Officer. Many were condemned and forcefully demolished. In 1900 about seventy-five houses were ordered to be demolished under stiff penalty for non-compliance.

A plague hospital was built in Britomart Street, designed to be burned down after it was no longer needed, and at the city destructor, 3d was paid for each dead rat brought in for burning — a procedure enthusiastically undertaken by schoolboys, who were easily persuaded to miss school in favour of earning handfuls of threepenny coins.

Epidemics put a lot of strain on the hospital building and administration, as did a curtailing of funding in the 1890s, which precluded any additional buildings except for an operating theatre in 1897. Most of the money for this came from public canvassing, done at the time of Queen Victoria's Diamond Jubilee and seen as a fitting memorial.

It was not until after the turn of the century that a number of new, desperately needed hospital buildings opened, catering for specific nursing needs. In 1904 the nurses' home was opened, signalling the arrival of a trained body of workers (a three-year training course had been instituted in 1895); in 1905 the Victoria Hospital for Chronic Diseases was opened; 1906 saw the opening of the publicly funded Seddon Ward for Consumptives; and in 1908 the Fever Hospital in Coromandel Street was opened.

The words 'incurable and chronic invalids' may sound harsh to twentieth-century ears, but in colonial life they accurately depicted a section of the population which, by its sheer presence, could not be ignored. Many diseases, conditions and accident injuries were incurable, and the results for the sufferers were often misery, poverty and abandonment. Some incurables were kept at home, but many had no relatives and were shuffled around the various institutions or left to fend for themselves.

Church agencies, particularly the Catholic Church and the Salvation Army, did much to assist. Of immense worth was Mother Suzanne Aubert's St Joseph's Home for Incurables, which opened its doors in 1900 in Buckle Street with much public support. It took its name from the nearby St Joseph's Catholic Church. In 1907 Mother Aubert moved to a new building at Island Bay, more widely known as the Home of Compassion than St Joseph's, and here she devoted herself to the care of incurables and foundlings.

The lunatic asylum in colonial New Zealand was an institution sometimes praised, often faulted, grudgingly funded, overcrowded and regularly used as a dumping ground for the feeble, the impoverished and the criminal. Under provincial government most major towns had asylums built and their inmates led a life of physical work and organised recreation. Wellington's asylum was opened in 1854 in the country at Karori and functioned for twenty years despite substandard buildings and a pervading sense of isolation and neglect. In 1872 Christian Toxward designed a new asylum at Mt View, a sloping plateau at the rear of the site of Newtown Hospital, which is where Government House now stands. The asylum opened its doors in 1873 with the transfer of patients from Karori: twenty-one males and forty-six females. The building could accommodate sixty comfortably, and a library and regular concerts were part of the relaxing therapy for its occupants. A certain public curiosity was aroused by the institution, enough to move the *New Zealand Mail* (November 1874) to report: 'the asylum . . . is almost, if not more than, as frequently visited as the museum.'

Toxward's building, however, could not keep up with the demand for space, as the economic depression and an ageing bachelor population (who had arrived as young pioneers three decades earlier) produced numbers of people seeking, or sent for, admission. Extensive additions were made to the asylum in 1883: two vast wings, one for males, one for females. But overcrowding, strained resources and some sensational newspaper reporting of conditions and cruelty prompted a Royal Commission to investigate the institution.

Among the more depressing features of the asylum reported were some out-houses used to incarcerate violent patients. They had high, barred windows, sloping floors for effluent run-off, doors with inspection holes and slots for pushing food through. Such features, coupled with a growing public fear of the asylum, led the government to buy a fifty-three-hectare farm at Porirua in 1884 for use as a major asylum. The move was paralleled in other cities with the purchase and construction of farm-asylums far from the centres of population. The site at Porirua was good farming land and remote, although accessible by way of the Wellington-Manawatu railway. Patients were moved here over a number of years, and by the time the last patients were moved out of Mt View in 1909, the foundations for the new Government House already stretched across the gardens in front of the old asylum.

SCHOOLING in pioneer Wellington was almost exclusively undertaken by private and church concerns. The private schools were small and often took only a handful of 'scholars', as the pupils were called. They were often just adjuncts to houses, and all charged fees. A census return for 1851 notes sixteen such schools in Wellington, with a total roll of nearly 600 pupils. They were run by people whose experience and lists of subjects available made interesting reading in their advertisements. Yet it was to these advertisements that the parents of prospective pupils might turn to aid their decision. For the greater part, the schools were elementary or 'infant' status, yet some of their names suggest grander hopes: Charles Grace's 'Wellington Academical Institution', Rev. Wheeler's 'Te Aro Grammar School', J. G. Grant's 'Wellington Academy, and C. D. de Castro's 'Kingsdown House Academy'.

The main church-sponsored schools of colonial Wellington were: the Anglican St Paul's School in Thorndon and St Peter's School in Ghuznee Street; the Catholic St Joseph's Industrial School in Hawkestone Street and St Mary's in Hill Street; and the Marist Brothers' School in Boulcott Street.

In 1871 the Wellington Provincial Council took over the organisation of primary education, and by 1875 had opened its first school for infants in Buckle Street. Others followed: the Terrace School (1875), Taranaki Street Boys' School (1878), Newtown School (1879), Thorndon School (1880), Willis Street School (1881), Clyde Quay School (1889) and Rintoul Street School (1896).

Secondary schooling was rare, despite repeated calls

for it. Wellington College was the best-known high school for years and although set out as a boys' school, it did admit girls for a brief spell. A Girls' High School opened in a small leased building in upper Abel Smith Street in 1883, a building which had hitherto been Thomas Bowden's 'English High School'. Although a fee-paying school, demand was such that its governors soon had to find larger premises. In 1887 the Wellington Girls' High School opened its doors in a fine building designed by Thomas Turnbull, who, incidentally, owned the Abel Smith Street building.

COLONIAL Wellington supplied its citizens with a variety of public recreation facilities. The emergence of libraries, museums, theatres, public reserves, meeting halls, sports grounds and baths were all signs that the city was indeed advancing. Yet these advances did not always come about smoothly. Battles over sites, designs, funding or even the purpose of a building hampered or prevented progress. The colonials regarded many of Wellington's facilities as makeshift and feeble compared with other cities, particularly the museum, public halls and the library. With restricted government grants, little income from agriculture, manufacturing or from resources like gold, coal and timber, and a paucity of benefactions from the wealthy, the degree of public donation in Wellington was admirable. Public donations greatly helped to fund everything from the public library to the Home for Incurables, from band rotundas to parish halls and from the statue of Queen Victoria to the children's hospital. Admission was charged to most places and events, and was often high enough to exclude the working classes, and definitely the impoverished.

One of the first notable buildings for public assembly was the Oddfellows Hall, built in 1859 on a small tongue of reclaimed land jutting out from Lambton Quay. From the street it presented a fairly handsome appearance, mainly because of the double-storeyed portico, an architectural device that could make any shed more noticeable. The hall was not only a popular and convenient meeting place for the public, but also the physical focus for the members of the Oddfellows Society. The meeting places of masonic lodges should not be underestimated when looking at the fabric of the country's settlements. They offered their members tradition, links with the past, mutual support and company.

Another early establishment was the Athenaeum and Mechanics' Institute, the forerunner of the public library. It offered night classes in practical subjects, lectures on discoveries, theories and scientific advances, and entertainments from visiting performers. The Athenaeum had already had two premises before it engaged Thomas Turnbull to design a striking building on Lambton Quay in 1876. It was built at a cost of £8,500, which was well over the sum borrowed for its construction. Its ground floor had shops for lease and a public lecture hall seating 500. Its first floor had the library, a reading room and a chess room, and its top floor had seven rooms for rent to local bodies.

Unfortunately the excessive borrowing forced the trustees of the institution to auction the building to pay debts. It went up for sale in 1888 and was bought by local entrepreneur and auctioneer Thomas Kennedy Macdonald (familiarly called Kennedy Mac by the press), who turned it into auction rooms and renamed it the Exchange. Macdonald leased back part of his purchase to the Athenaeum and they stayed in the building until the opening of the new public library in 1893.

Lobbying for a free (as opposed to subscription) library for the city had been underway for some time, but the project needed a catalyst. This was provided in 1889 by local merchant William Levin, who offered the city £1,000 towards the building on condition that public fundraising met the balance and that work started within fifteen months. The city met Levin's challenge, and all kinds of fundraising were embarked upon. Among these was the opening to the public (for a charge of 6d a head) of the Union Company's new luxury steamer *Monowai*, an event that produced a contribution of £10. The Wirth Brothers' Circus also donated their proceeds to the fund.

In 1890 the City Council advertised a design competition for a building of £10,000, with provision to allow the erection of one wing initially to a maximum cost of £4,000. Twenty-two entries were received and the winner was William Crichton, who had just arrived in Wellington to work as assistant to the Government Architect. Crichton's design was so unusual in style that the established architects of the city found it hard to accept.

Francis Penty, the third prize winner, criticised Crichton's design because it was sent in on wrong-sized paper and had been coloured in. Penty also damned the second prize winner, Thomas Turnbull, for producing a design that was patently too expensive for the amount stipulated.

The building was opened in 1893 and, with later additions, remained the public library until the opening of the new Central Library in 1940.

THE larger New Zealand cities often gathered the nucleus of their museum collections in the early years of settlement, although priority was not always given to housing them. The collections focused to a large extent on natural history, although ethnography also held an important place. The museum collections served both public interest and scientific research. Research was a major catalyst for collecting, exchange and the publication of reports. This scientific interest in the new country spurred the formation of the New Zealand Society (much later the Royal Society), which held its first meeting in the Athenaeum on Lambton Quay in 1851. This group, along with some highly skilled amateurs who had a strong interest in a geological survey of the country, led the government to establish the Colonial Museum in Wellington. It was built in 1864 near Parliament House, fronting a small street later called Museum Street. The building was particularly plain and not very secure, and within a year it was visited by burglars who carried off items worth £200. 'From the lone position of the building, and its unprotected state, without a caretaker on the premises or any guard whatever, the wonder is it remained so long without being pillaged,' announced the *Evening Post* in February 1866.

Because of its status as a statutory body, the museum

received government money, allowing it to increase its collections and library and publish occasional papers. In 1875 a new wing, gallery and double-storeyed office and library block was added to the museum, all designed by William Clayton. This addition was to last until the museum (now called the Dominion Museum) moved into its current premises on Mt Cook in the late 1930s. After the move was completed, Clayton's building was demolished in 1939 to make way for a Broadcasting House, which did not eventuate until the late 1950s. The attendance figures attest to the Colonial Museum's popularity. Its numerous acquisitions and gifts, and the hosting of important conferences and overseas visitors suggest it was a lively and influential institution.

ON the first town map of Wellington a vast tract of land called the Town Belt, spreading from Thorndon to Mt Victoria, was reserved for public enjoyment. While this was a move of some consequence, it had the effect of hemming the town in, and later created a line of demarkation between the city and its suburbs. Although the belt provided a large area of open space, provision for small parks within the city was negligible. In October 1906 the *Evening Post* commented that '[a few] tiny triangles, with two or three larger areas whose shape has no name in geometry, remain as a monument to pioneer thoughtlessness'.

In 1844, part of the Town Belt was designated the Botanic Garden, but it took about another thirty years before sufficient money and resources became available to develop it. When it was finally established as a recreational, educational and research amenity, it became very popular. Over the years, its thirty-one hectares have seen many changes in terms of function and fashion.

The Botanic Garden was not the only public recreational amenity. Colonial Wellington also had private pleasure and tea gardens, often run by experienced gardeners who imported a vast array of plants and whose professional association with the Botanic Garden was as close as it was mutually beneficial. Among the well-known private pleasure gardens were Wilkinson's on Oriental Bay, Donald's in Karori and Bellevue in the Hutt.

WITH such easy access to the harbour, swimming and boating were popular activities, albeit tinged with the possibility of danger and accident. From the 1850s there were calls for public swimming baths to provide supervision and to minimise the danger of shark attack and unnoticed currents in the sea. The first baths were the Te Aro baths along what is now Oriental Parade, and now the site of the Freyberg Pool. Essentially these baths were an area of high-tide beach cordoned off by a fence of totara piles, with a few sheds for changing rooms and refreshments. Nevertheless, the baths had an architect — A. A. G. Pilmer — and the *Wellington Independent* noted with some comfort that the piles were spaced 'so that ample security is afforded that only the smaller fish can enter' (December 1864). The Te Aro baths were replaced with a finer building designed by the City Engineer in 1901.

Moves to establish a public pool at the other end of the town came to fruition when Charles Tringham designed the Thorndon Baths in 1874. Again, it was another area fenced off from the sea. It was replaced in 1898 by a splendid new building designed by Joshua Charlesworth, which proved very popular. Soon the foreshore on which it was built was beautified by planting, paths, seats and a band rotunda, forming the Thorndon Esplanade. However, all this was subsequently swept away by massive reclamations.

THE building of a town hall often provided a social focus and epitomised, through its architecture, all that was progressive, confident and enterprising about a city. In short, it was the jewel in the civic crown. Yet many New Zealand cities had to wait for decades before a town hall was built. Delays were caused by insufficient funding, shifts in priority, and battles over sites. It was more than sixty years — well into the third generation of settlement — before construction began on Wellington's Town Hall, with its dual function of council offices and large public auditorium.

Thomas Turnbull had designed council offices in Featherston Street in 1877, but these housed just the City Council and had no public function. The mayor and several local musical bodies started lobbying for a real town hall in the late 1890s. Financing was not seen as insurmountable, for the users would pay and the council leaseholds in the central city would provide ongoing income. In 1900 the Council's Finance Committee recommended the Town Hall proceed. They held a design competition, which drew thirteen entries, and the winner, Joshua Charlesworth, was announced early in 1901. Interest in the building was so great that the entries were exhibited publicly, even though most of them were vastly in excess of requirements and some horribly expensive. With the visit of the Duke and Duchess of Cornwall and York to Wellington imminent, tenders were called just for the hall's foundations so that the Duke would have somewhere to lay the foundation stone.

Construction went slowly and modifications were made along the way. The building, costing £68,000, was ready for opening in December 1904. On opening day the front was festooned with flags and electric bulbs, and the crowds spread into Cuba Street and blocked the trams. The mayor opened the building with a golden key and treated the audience inside to a speech on the history of the city. Later that night the first musical concert was held in the Town Hall.

THE establishment of clubs and societies, whether social, sporting, military or political, is a feature typical of most human settlements. Wellington had a large range of clubs including the Wellington Club (for gentlemen), the Society for the Preservation of Scenery, the Early Closing Movement (aimed at shops that remained open well into the night), the Anti-Asiatic League, the Star Boating Club and the Commercial Travellers' and Warehousemen's Club. They provided recreation and social bonding. Many clubs built premises contributing much to the appearance of the city. They also affected the city's development in material and cultural ways.

The Wellington Club provided its gentlemen members with accommodation and social facilities and

For the Public Good

was perhaps the most selective club in town. Before moving to its premises on the Terrace, its home was a building on Lambton Quay that had started life as a hotel in the mid-1840s. The club took over the building in the 1850s and it was sold in 1876 by the trustees to an ironmonger, who called in William Chatfield to alter the building, soon to be known as the Victoria Building.

THE arrival of overseas visitors in colonial Wellington was a cause for celebration, and no visitors were more welcome than royalty, particularly British royalty. In 1869 Queen Victoria's son Prince Alfred paid the colony a visit and was fêted throughout his few days' stay in Wellington. The 1901 Royal Tour of the Duke and Duchess of Cornwall and York aroused even more interest. They also spent only a few days in Wellington but were treated to a round of engagements including ministerial receptions, the laying of the foundation stone for the Town Hall and visits to the factories of Petone. They also attended more informal events such as the large bazaar held to raise funds for the Victoria Home for Incurables. It was billed as a 'Maori bazaar', with each stall called by a Maori name and decorated in Maori motifs. Close to £3,000 was raised, an amount that would easily buy a large house on Oriental Parade.

Another type of visitor that captivated the city's imagination was the theatrical, circus or opera troupe. They usually stayed just one night in Wellington on a countrywide or Australasian tour. Among the first to visit the capital of Wellington was an American circus called 'Bird, Blow and Wills'. They performed on the reclaimed land near the Oddfellows Hall in 1869. 'The entertainment last night was of the usual average,' reported the *Evening Post* in November 1869.

After the circus came an exhibition of Chang the giant (the tallest man in the world!) and Kin Foo (the first Chinese lady to be presented to Queen Victoria). It was held at the Empire Hotel, and the admission charge of 2s was exorbitant in 1870. In 1880 a huge circus played for five days in the paddocks of John Martin's estate in Vivian Street, a circus billed as reproducing 'All Earth's Greatest Marvels' under electric light. What could be seen was the 'only seven-horse rider living', six well-trained horses who could sit in chairs, march like soldiers and form tableaux, 650 feet of crawling reptiles and '1,000 thrilling novelties'.

Such shows may have provided exceptional entertainment, but for day-to-day living, the press firmly remarked that Wellington was 'singularly barren of all intellectual amusement . . . with the exception of flying visits from small companies of travelling performers or singers, there is really nothing to be called public entertainments — no place where an hour or two can be whiled away in the evening but the inevitable billiard-room or drinking saloon' (*Evening Post*, October 1869).

Exhibitions and celebrations were also enjoyed by the public and colonial Wellington was full of these. The monarch's birthday, the anniversary regatta, company employees' excursions, the laying of foundation stones and the ceremonial opening of buildings were all public affairs that drew large crowds. Buildings were often fabulously decorated on such occasions and the streets were lined with people.

Colonial Capital

Great crowds turned out to send off contingents to the Boer War from 1899 onwards. The first camp was established at Karori in late 1899, and here the men organised their equipment and horses, and possibly wondered how they would spend their 4s per day allowance. The First Contingent left on Saturday, 21 October 1899 on the troopship *Waiwera*, which had arrived from Lyttelton the previous night laden with food and with the carpenters still making the horse stalls. Friday night was declared a 'general leave' night for the troops, who went into town. Town that night was packed, and the local police were instructed to make suitable allowances for the 'agitated state of the public mind.' The troops were sent off on the Saturday from Queen's Wharf, an event to which every mayor in the country had been invited, with the cost of the telegrams waived by the Post Office. The Contingent marched down from Karori and were given a rousing send-off by about 40,000 onlookers. Thousands of flags and streamers decorated the streets, and local businesses donated comforts (including a piano). The soldiers were greeted by an official party on a specially built grandstand on the wharf and, after the ship pushed off, a flotilla of boats accompanied them to the harbour heads.

O F all the expenditure necessary to ensure the running of a city, perhaps the most unnoticed is that devoted to amenities. The provision of drainage, rubbish collection, road surfacing, gas reticulation and the like was unavoidable, and was as expensive as it was unglamorous. Such works often required loans to be raised and additional rates to be levied. To do this, the mandate of the city's ratepayers might have to be sought.

The need for roading in colonial Wellington was urgent almost from the outset. It continued to be pressing as the population and heavy traffic increased. Street lines had been delineated on the first town maps, but their carefully ruled lines bore little resemblance to the chaos and approximations of their physical state. The mud and dust provided material for perennial comment in the press. In 1873 the mud of Willis Street was described as a 'dusky compound varying between thick batter and thin gruel in consistency' (*Evening Post*, July 1873), while the holes in the roads provided good copy for letters to the editor. A correspondent to the *Wellington Omnibus* in August 1875 mentioned coming across a hole in Willis Street 'deep enough to bury the Mayor and two or three of his colts.'

The roads were made worse by litter and traffic. The litter included offensive matter which was later obviated by drainage and rubbish collection schemes. An outraged writer to the *Evening Post* in December 1875 reported seeing a servant girl throw a bucket of slops onto Lambton Quay from an upper floor window. The practice of turfing dead rats into the street was also roundly condemned, and dozens of them lying about daily were 'putrefying and emitting most poisonous effluvia' (*Evening Post*, December 1877). As for the reclaimed land yet to be built on, there were 'among the sweet-smelling and savoury items . . . the heads, bones and other offal of fish, night-soil, rotten cabbage leaves and other abominations' (*Evening Post*, April 1877).

The droving of mobs of cattle through the streets

also became a nuisance to comment on, and after observing one such mob the *Evening Post* thought that while this mob was unusually quiet 'it does not follow that the custom is a proper one' (October 1867). There was also the dangerous habit of tethering horses to verandah posts where they might move up onto the footpath. Thus 'passers by may choose between crawling under the horse's head at the risk of a bite, pushing round by his tail at the still greater risk of a kick, or slipping off the footpath into the mud' (*Evening Post*, August 1875).

Drainage of the city proved among the most expensive and challenging tasks facing the authorities, who also faced hostile criticism when its existing state was brought to public notice. 'It has been reported,' decried the *New Zealand Mail* in August 1874, 'but we can scarcely believe it to be true, that the night-carts of the City are now emptied on the Te Aro beach, near the mouth of the large drain which pours its filth into the harbour not far from the baths'. Drainage certainly was haphazard, and the first large-scale rectification of this began in 1879. An English engineer, Mr Clark, who had spent some years in New Zealand, prepared an extensive plan in 1878. The Council raised a £50,000 loan to put it into effect. Clark's scheme collected the city's sewerage and channelled it through a gravity-fed tunnel from Adelaide Road to the Owhiro Bay outfall. It was the first of many schemes, all of which needed sanctions to raise loans.

Rubbish collection also required effort and expenditure. By the 1880s the Council was tendering out 'scavenging rights' to contractors, who collected domestic rubbish in carts and took it to the city destructor on Clyde Quay. The rubbish-cart horses had bells fixed to their collars to alert citizens so they could put the rubbish out. The destructor, which soon had the city morgue erected next to it, was built in 1888. The construction of its thirty-seven metre chimney was watched with consternation by the residents of Mt Victoria, who suspected it would belch forth vast clouds of smoke — which it did, even though the engineers had promised they would see, at most, only 'a little vapour'.

The destructor was continually in action. Such was the volume of rubbish processed that the ash was packaged and sold as fertiliser. The larger 'clinkers' were thrown into the harbour — to aid the reclamations.

The city's footpaths provided subject for sharp comment and various methods were tried to improve them. One method was to paint them with tar and sprinkle them with sand and broken shells. By far the best method was to pave them with large tiles of Caithness stone, a venture that started in the late 1870s. Half of the cost was met by the owners of premises fronting the paths. Lambton Quay was flagged by the early 1880s, but not before Customhouse Quay was completed. 'But then,' pointed out the *Evening Post* (January 1880), 'there are two banks and an insurance company's office in Customhouse Quay which no doubt makes a difference.'

WALKING was the dominant mode of private transport in the early years of Wellington. Moves to provide the city with public transport were made as early as 1873, when enterprising engineer Charles O'Neill applied to the City Council to lay tram tracks from Cuba Street to Molesworth Street. The scheme was to be privately funded, and three years later the prospectus for the Wellington City Tramways Company was launched. The first engines were cumbersome steam boilers that operated for four years before being replaced by horses. The company changed hands several times. It had two directorates before being bought by well-connected physician Morgan Grace and leased to veteran transport operator Archibald Hall, who managed to run it at a profit for the first time. In 1900 the City Council bought the tramways from the company — all property and stock — for close to £20,000, the price arrived at by arbitration. The City Council undertook to electrify the system in stages from 1902, a venture which cost £55,000 and which had been suggested as early as 1896.

The 1870s were a decade of vast expenditure on rail transport in New Zealand, and Wellington, being a major terminus and shipping port, was to share in this network. The first rail link out of the city was to the Hutt Valley, as part of the Wellington to Masterton line. Work on it had begun in the winter of 1872 and was inaugurated with a splendid ball for 500 at the Theatre Royal and a midnight supper laid out on the theatre's stage. Work on this thirteen-kilometre stretch was hampered by heavy sea swells, swollen mountain streams and the need to build the track on an embankment. It was opened in April 1874, but without any ceremony. 'About twenty gentlemen, a large number of small boys and two Maori women assembled to see the departure of the first train,' recorded the *Evening Post* in April 1874, 'but their enthusiasm was not sufficient to give a cheer as the train moved off with the passengers, most of whom were juveniles.'

In 1882 a private company was formed to build a new rail link between Wellington and the Manawatu. It was opened in late 1886 with a train whose 'passengers' consisted of sixty cattle and 345 sheep. Both the government and the Manawatu railway lines worked adjacent for a number of years before being amalgamated in 1908.

Good street lighting was an amenity any city of size wished to possess. Before gas became available, the only street lighting was that provided by the burning of lamps outside the entrance to every hotel — a service demanded by law. Gas lighting came to the city in 1871 and was used for both street standards and building interiors. Electricity made its debut in the city in 1883 with the lighting of the Government Printing Office with sixty-five lights. The building was opened to the public so they could see the event. Full street lighting by electricity started in 1889, when the lights went on in the city's Lambton Ward.

Provision also had to be made for burying the dead. Colonial Wellington's cemetery was noted for its chequered history. The cemetery area of about seven hectares (later known as the Bolton Street Cemetery) had been pencilled in on the early town map and divided up for use by Anglicans, non-Anglicans and Jews, with the Roman Catholics having their own cemetery near what today is Mount Street. This division was

For the Public Good

a source of discontent from the outset. Further discontent followed as the cemetery became overcrowded and the problems of a central city site became apparent. In the 1850s it was a forlorn place — hilly, scrubby, windswept and grazed by stock. Most of the graves were only discernible by their white picket fences. By the 1860s the cemetery was increased in size, making it harder to shift it than before. 'It was a great mistake even to place it in the position it occupies,' lamented the *Evening Post* in December 1866, 'but it is still a greater one to go on increasing its area.'

In 1890 the City Council, after having advertised for suitable land, chose to relocate the cemetery on a thirty-eight hectare site at Karori, which it bought for £4,000. While the purchase was instrumental in opening up the suburb with an improved road, it was also fuelled by a strong public dissatisfaction with the health hazards and fearful condition of the existing cemetery.

Patterns of Settlement

THE steady increase in Wellington's population hastened progress in fields such as commerce, public buildings, amenities and the physical appearance of the city. Population figures for Wellington during its colonial period record an increase of about 1,000 per year.

Settlement in pioneer Wellington arranged itself close to the beach and on the flats of Te Aro and Thorndon, close to the commercial centres of town and near the wharves and jetties. It was a reasonable pattern, considering most people walked everywhere and the population was small. Domestic architecture of this pre-capital period was typified by the small wooden hut with shingled roofs and tiny windows. Often built right up to the line of the footpaths (or the footpaths to be), few of these huts had more than three or four rooms, with sleeping quarters in the attics quite common. Most were built with timber milled from the forests that clothed the hills around the harbour. However, a handful of cottages had come to New Zealand as prefabricated parts on board ship. Timber was milled close to the town with an almost fierce greed, and it was not long before demand for wood could only be met by the sawmills established in the Wairarapa in the 1870s. Wood was not only the dominant building material, but was also the only ready source of fuel and fencing.

By the time Wellington was declared the capital, most of the population lived on the two flats. As the population increased with the city's new status and the extensive immigration in the 1870s, these flats still retained their popularity for domestic residences. The slopes of Mt Victoria and the Terrace area also became peppered with numerous houses.

For many decades after colonisation Oriental Bay was deemed more out of the way than desirable, with its then-rocky beach, rough track and steep hills. However, the town's first private pleasure garden (Wilkinson's) was established here on a site now bisected by Grass Street. By the late 1870s a number of sizeable houses, referred to in advertisements as 'marine villas', had been built along Oriental Parade. By the 1890s much infill building had turned the bay into a popular area for both residents and visitors. The few straggling paths up the steep hills were formed into roads and their land subdivided for house sites. By the turn of the century the bay was well populated and soon became an inner city suburb with the opening up of the Roseneath estate, which was subdivided into seventy different-sized sections for sale at about £100 each. Also contributing to its popularity was the tram service, and the building of houses on sites once avoided for their difficulty. For example, Joshua Charlesworth called tenders in 1906 for eight elaborate villas he designed for a stretch of the Parade nestling underneath a large cliff called FitzGerald's Point.

Although the establishment of suburbs around the turn of the century provided much scope for expansion, it did not leave the Thorndon and Te Aro flats in the doldrums. By this time many of the larger estates had been broken up and their street frontages were subdivided for new house building. Such infill building was not just limited to single houses here and there, but was often done by the handful, which suggested demand for inner city housing was still strong. Architects might find themselves calling tenders for rows of houses for developers. The houses were of better quality than the developers' styles of the 1870s.

Redevelopment also could result in new streets or the upgrading of rough tracks or rights of way. In Mt Victoria pleasant new streets such as Porritt Avenue (then called Ellice Avenue), Armour Avenue (then called Brougham Avenue) and Claremont Grove were established. In the 1900s some of Thorndon's grand estates were subdivided and villa sites advertised for sale. Examples of this were: Hawkestone Crescent (a division of J. B. Harcourt's estate); Portland Crescent (a division of Dr Grace's estate); Burnell Avenue (a division of the W. H. Levin estate); and Hobson Crescent, a green area of about one hectare off Hobson Street, which had been suggested as a site for a public domain but was snapped up by David Ziman of South Africa in 1895 and subdivided into twenty-seven house sites. Conditions were imposed on these redevelopments. For example, there was a restriction on house density to preclude slums, and no commercial or business premises were to be allowed.

Nevertheless, the domestic nature of the inner city flat land was not to be maintained indefinitely. Commercial, industrial and other concerns were soon to make significant inroads, and eventually these areas were designated non-residential. Commerce had annexed much of Thorndon's arterial Molesworth Street, and by the First World War, many of Te Aro's main thoroughfares and small connecting streets were well populated with shops and warehouses. Manufacturing, one of the major employers of the 1900s, also found the Te Aro flat a convenient location and such concerns as Hannah's boot factory and Bryant's match factory tended to displace the domestic nature of the area.

In general, a suburb is more than a domestic area set away from the city centre. It often has its own services such as shops, schools, churches and industry. The topography, siting, and the quality of its buildings and amenities give it its own particular 'character'.

The area called Newtown was present on the original Town Acre maps of the city, and it seems reasonable to call it the city's first suburb. Its progress for the first few decades of settlement was unspectacular. Yet by the 1880s it was beginning to take on a busy appearance, and by the turn of the century it was one of the most densely populated areas of the country. The location of the city's hospital in Newtown provided an impetus for expansion, as did the establishment of small industry. Further visible promotion of the area came with the building of shops along the main streets. By the turn of the century, main-street Newtown was a thriving commercial precinct. Access to Newtown was by tram, and the placing of the tram terminus, workshops and stables in the suburb assured it a continued link with the city centre. Demand for house sites led to subdivision and prosperous building activity, on both a small and large scale.

Perhaps the most heralded subdivision scheme in Newtown was the auctioning of twenty-two acres (about nine hectares), the property of merchant William Turnbull, as 238 house sites. Called the Wellesley Block (named after the Duke of Wellington), publicity for this sale included the printing of large posters complete with a map of the sections and a plethora of letterpress extolling the area for its drainage, sunlight, quietude and good street frontages. However, the auction, held in 1889, resulted in only one section being sold, and the rest went up for private sale. The initial response to the auction may have been disappointing, but then this period was flooded with enthusiastically billed auctions of house sites, including 206 sections in Brooklyn (1888), 105 sections in Karori (1888), 212 sites in Kelburn (1900) and 104 sites in Karori (1904). All these competed with auctions of numerous townships in both the Wairarapa and up the line into the Horowhenua.

Rich and Poor

THE wealthy of colonial Wellington, like the wealthy of the rest of the country, were not numerically strong, but they were powerful when it came to matters of politics, business and social leadership. The two potential generators of large wealth were commerce and land, areas embracing farming, property speculation, manufacturing, monopoly merchandising and warehousing. To establish oneself successfully in these fields, one required starting capital. This prerequisite tended to preclude the majority of colonists. Apart from capital, the possession of education, contacts and financial acumen could only but assist the path to wealth.

In colonial Wellington the ownership of land — especially central city commercial land — provided a handful of investors with phenomonal results. Increases in value of 100 percent over a few months were not unknown in the boom times of the 1870s. Coupled with land ownership was the development of properties for commercial rental purposes which provided immediate income over and above the capital gain collected on selling. Among the more assiduous private developers of colonial Wellington were Jacob Joseph, Sarah Rhodes, John Martin, Thomas Macarthy, Samuel Gilmer and Martin Kennedy.

Wealth from retailing was evident in colonial Wellington but it was not necessarily the rule. The wealthy retailers had generally established themselves within the first few decades of the town's settlement and had gained the trust and patronage of their customers. They dealt in popular, almost essential lines and their ambitions were all but monopolistic. People like John Kirkcaldie, James Smith and Edward Anderson attained wealth through such techniques as progressive retailing, inventive advertising, the opening of branch premises, and generating demand and expansion.

Dealing in commodities such as coal, grain, iron and timber was closely related to retailing. Warehousing and importing went hand in hand with retail and commodities trading. Here again, early establishment and a monopolistic stance were advantageous. People like John Johnston, Joseph Nathan, Walter Turnbull, William Bannatyne and George Shannon had plenty to show for their enterprises and plenty to leave to their children. Manufacturing was another field that could return notable wealth, although it was also notorious for failure. The eminent manufacturers of colonial Wellington included Robert Hannah, Edward Mills, James Gear and Henry Blundell, all of whose enterprises were well underway by the 1870s. These fields should not be considered mutually exclusive, as cross-involvement was common among the wealthy. They were often placed on the directorate of existing companies and of companies being formed and open to public subscription. Indeed, the obituaries of many of the city's wealthy are so filled with bewildering lists of the commercial directorships they held that there is scarcely room for any other social or personal record.

One of the most visible manifestations of wealth, apart from imposing business premises, was 'the big house' and it set the wealthy apart from the rest of the town's citizenry more than anything else. The golden age of building such houses in Wellington was from the late 1870s until the turn of the century. Houses of more than fifteen rooms, requiring the services of three or four staff and set in grounds of about one hectare were built to the tune of around £3,000 — about ten times the amount a labourer might be faced with when buying a small three-roomed cottage on a small section. The wealthy of Wellington did not achieve some of the fantastic houses that the merchants of Auckland or the station-holders of Canterbury and Otago built, but they stood well out from the rest of Wellington's houses.

The house built for merchant John Johnston in Fitzherbert Terrace in 1875 was one of the most notable in Wellington. Designed by Thomas Turnbull, its formal appearance and wealth of detailing were softened by its setting in generous gardens, lawns and bush that extended back to, and mingled with, the grounds of Thomas Williams's stately home in Hobson Street, with its observation tower. (This is now the nucleus of Queen Margaret College.) The Johnston residence was one of the first big houses in Wellington. One of the later houses was the extraordinary concrete structure 'Moana Lua', built for Robert Levin in 1902 in Hobson Street and designed by John Swan. It was a wedding present to Robert Levin's wife (Norah Riddiford) but within five years of its construction the Levins had sold it and moved to the Manawatu. The new owner was Ian Duncan, son of a prominent importer and a director of the family concern Levin and Co.

'The big house' could certainly be considered a barometer of wealth, but there were many other areas of life in which the wealthy could make a display of their position, influence and comfort. Among these was private transport. Owning a splendid rig like a landau or a brougham immediately set you apart from the crowd. Even more dashing was having your own coachman, although this was not common. The advent of the motorcar also provided the wealthy an opportunity to exhibit their status. The first car seen in Wellington had its test run up and down Victoria Street (reaching a speed of 20 m.p.h.) in 1898. It was a Benz imported in parts from Paris and made up at Seager's Foundry. It was not long before the car captivated the attention of the city's well-heeled and within a few years some powerful machines were seen around town.

A more sedate display of success could be made in the field of private entertainment. The private ballroom was a distinguishing feature par excellence, although few houses possessed one. Perhaps the most notable one was that of the Hon. Walter Johnston on Tinakori Road, later moved to Goring Street and used as a public hall.

However, large rooms could easily suffice as ballrooms, and one of the most ardent dance-givers of late colonial Wellington was Miss Emily Johnston of Fitz-

Rich and Poor

herbert Terrace. Well noted for her elaborate floral decorations, Emily Johnston was also renowned for her moonlight dances. On one occasion in December 1903 the front lawn of her house was built over with a wooden dance floor, the house draped with strings of coloured electric lights and the grounds filled with groups of furniture and refreshment stations. Mrs T. C. Williams in nearby Hobson Street was also noted for her private dances. The house's large hall had a gallery on the first floor that provided a useful vantage point for chaperones. The town's hairdressers were booked up all afternoon and Hobson Street jammed with smart rigs, as the result of one of Mrs Williams's larger entertainments in February 1897. She had two orchestras in attendance for the occasion, one stationed inside and the other outside. The presence of the Governor and his wife added to the splendour of the function.

Big houses, cars and private dances were some of the extrovert features of the life of the wealthy. Other aspects of wealth that fostered eminence were overseas trips, intermarriage with other 'leading' families and financial involvement in sport (especially racing) and charities.

One of the many sources of government revenue was a tax on the net value of a deceased estate – the death duty. A glance at the values of estates shows the polarity between the wealthy and the poor. Many working class people left very little or nothing on their deaths and were thus exempt from estate duty. Most deceased estates attracted duty of about a few hundred pounds. However, the value of the estates of the wealthy was enormous by comparison. For example, W. B. Rhodes (1882) was valued at £273,000; W. H. Levin (1893) at £243,000; Walter Turnbull (1897) at £120,000; Jacob Joseph (1903) at £291,000; W. W. Johnston (1907) at £497,000; and E. J. Riddiford (1911) at £585,000. In the case of Jacob Joseph, his estate value was about 30,000 times the average working wage. The majority of people must have stood in some awe of these figures, which were regularly published in the country's newspapers.

COLONIAL Wellington society was marked by a great polarity of the rich and the poor. There were many poor people in the city, and many causes and manifestations of poverty. One potent cause of poverty was unemployment, especially when the unemployed had no resources to fall back on and state aid was all but unavailable. Unemployment was rife in the late 1870s and until the turn of the century. It was caused both by a commercial depression that laid off hundreds, and a large increase in population arising from government-funded immigration. These 'new chums', as they were called by the press, arrived to find no work and no housing provided for them. A return to England was, for most, impossible. The *Evening Post* in September 1879 made ironic and punchy comment on the continuing arrival of immigrants, hoping that the working men of Wellington might 'appreciate the efforts of Sir George Grey's Government to provide them with ample competition lest they should wax fat by reason of their high wages.' The unemployed (sometimes referred to by the phrase the 'bone and sinew') were not generally organised and often found they had little sympathy from the general public or the press. On one occasion they called a grievance meeting, to be held at the top of

Mt Victoria. Although few turned up, the press had a fine time reporting it. They asked why Mt Victoria had been chosen, 'for after climbing such a distance . . . it can hardly be said that any person in the meeting can be considered unemployed' (*New Zealand Mail*, February 1880).

A further meeting was called in front of the railway station. The only conceivable way to alleviate their situation was by petitioning the government for relief. At this time, it was estimated by the Government Relieving Officer who reported to the Colonial Treasurer that there were about 600 unemployed men in Wellington — about ten percent of the male workforce. The figure tends to disguise the fact that these men had many dependents, and a reluctance to 'register' as unemployed meant the statistic was very much a minimum.

Another cause of poverty was low wages, particularly if there was only one wage-earner in the family, and where these wages represented long hours. Little wonder house ownership was not widely achieved by many of Wellington's population. The alternative was to rent. The low quality of rental accommodation for the poor was brought to public notice through the press and the reports of the benevolent agencies. At its fiercest, the depression straddling the late 1870s and early 1880s led to such appalling conditions as overcrowding (one family per room not being unusual), the spread of infectious diseases, and the building of hovels along narrow private streets ungoverned by health, fire or building inspection, but reaping plump profits for their developers. Among the many private streets to come before public notice was Little Taranaki Street (now Egmont Street off Dixon Street), which the *Evening Post*, in October 1876, referred to as a 'perfect sink of filth and hotbed of disease'. It resembled a charnel house with masses of bones and animal matter lying around. The tenants sometimes took in hospital laundry to wash for money, and there were poultices and dressings lying about the street until they were carried away by roaming dogs. A complaint in the press (November 1877) about dense subdivision noted up to thirty houses per acre in Lorne Street — as dense as a London suburb — with no drainage, so slops were simply thrown out and the land was saturated.

Some appalling housing conditions were reported during the depression. One press article recounted a family of nine living in two Alpha Street rooms whose dimensions, in terms of cubic feet per person, were half the lowest limit allowed by London's Poor Law Board (*Evening Post*, July 1876). Developers of such housing were held in low esteem and were known as 'carcase-builders'.

Privately surveyed narrow streets became a burning issue for the City Council, who eventually moved to regulate their dimensions, densities and services. Over seventy such streets existed in central Wellington, and the Council proposed to take them over — where petitioned to — and improve them.

In one instance of slum clearance, the tenants of one small street, Cambridge Road, petitioned the Council to rename their street to remove its stigma when it was rebuilt in 1899. The Council did so and the street, off Cambridge Terrace, is known today by its new name, Tennyson Street.

Rich and Poor

The reports of how the poor lived made some interesting social comments. Many of poverty's victims had been in the country for only a few months. It was found that many people could obtain only sporadic work, whether they were skilled tradesmen or domestic servants. The steep rent and need for food led many people to sell virtually everything, including clothes and furniture. Subletting rooms and out-houses was widespread and almost unavoidable. The aid offered by the Benevolent Trustees was often only sought as a final measure.

Homelessness was also a problem. At its peak in the late 1890s the Harbour Board fitted up one of its sheds as a night shelter to prevent the homeless from being thrown into prison for vagrancy. Bunks were made up in tiers and to pay for board, the men were required to work at stone-breaking during the day. In the 1890s soup kitchens were set up in Courtenay Place, open for lunch six days a week with a charge of 2d a pint for those who had money but no charge for the destitute. In 1899 the Salvation Army opened a workingman's hotel in Buckle Street, the first in New Zealand, with beds for 8d a night or 'fourpenny dossers' of straw mattresses on bunks. For those with no money, the usual exchange of labour for accommodation was expected.

An increase in crime further illuminated the human face of the depression. While steep rents and low wages may well be construed as crimes, it was not these that filled the charge sheets in the Resident Magistrate's and Supreme Courts. It was theft, vagrancy, bankruptcy, assault, disturbing the peace and suchlike. Many of these charges were dealt with summarily in the press, while more serious crimes such as infanticide and the running of brothels received disproportionate press coverage.

Editorials spoke of the rise in suicide as phenomenal and added stern condemnation of it, calling it a luxury and those contemplating it should remember that their bodies would be 'consigned with marks of their ignominy to unknown graves' (*Evening Post*, July 1885). As attempted suicide was a crime, those charged with it were brought before the courts. In 1884 one such hapless case was charged and sentenced to a bond of £100 to keep the peace towards himself. A week later he committed suicide and his body was found in the harbour. Like many destitute people, he was single and had no relatives in the country.

The most common method of suicide for a few years was the taking of a hideous preparation called Rough on Rats, available from any chemist. An arsenical compound, it was effective, although death was agonising and slow.

As for the world of prostitution, it was generally agreed (both by law and by social usage) that being a prostitute *per se* was not a crime, but the keeping of brothels or 'disorderly houses' was. It was also generally agreed that Wellington's prostitutes made more public display of their work than those in any other city. Parading around in carriages and laden with jewellery, they became models for poverty-stricken young women who saw this as their only means of making money. This cause-and-effect unfortunately trapped very young girls, and the records of the Salvation Army, who ran 'rescue homes', show many girls aged as young as eleven becoming involved.

Attempts were made to eradicate prostitution by a number of means. One method was to invoke an old statute from the reign of Charles II; another was an interpretation of the Contagious Diseases Act, and there was always the action of making complaint to the police. The Carolean statute was employed in 1883 by a number of people living in Dixon Street to rid themselves of a brothel there. The brothel owner was committed for trial, charged with keeping a disorderly house and sentenced to keep the peace for a year with a surety of £50. The success of this conviction led others to prosecute, and by the turn of the century the brothels, while still in existence, were out of the public spotlight as far as the press was concerned.

One of Wellington's more notorious brothel-busting episodes came in August 1887 when a police raid in Ghuznee Street revealed a spectacle scarcely believable. Dubbed the 'Rabbit Burrows', it was a collection of six hovels, each only a metre and a half high, their floors swilling in human filth and the occupants sleeping in sacks. It was run by a man who depended on his daughters' prostitution for an income, and whose two sons (aged ten and twelve) were charged with being children living with prostitutes, that is, with their sisters. The man was sent to prison for three months while the children were sent away to industrial schools in the South Island until they turned fifteen.

The brothels themselves were more often run-down houses in streets of depressed character. They tended to be rented and their owners might be established members of society who knew that prostitutes could better afford the rent than the unemployed. The magazine *Fair Play* in November 1893 strongly suggested that the landlords' names should be published in the papers. Most of Thorndon's brothels were in tiny Fraser's Lane and John Street, while the south end of town had a brothel 'precinct' around Quin (later Sturdee) and Ghuznee Streets. In 1885 police returns showed Wellington had twenty brothels with about sixty prostitutes, the majority of them living in Thorndon.

A FURTHER manifestation of poverty was the use of a racial scapegoat in the Chinese. 'John Chinaman', as the press collectively termed the Chinese, was roundly disliked for undercutting European shopowners' prices, for employing family members, for gathering together in ghettos, for opium smoking and gambling dens. The dislike was evident in any city in which the Chinese settled, yet as a proportion of the population they were a small minority. By the 1870s moves were afoot to pressurise the government to stop the influx of what was termed a 'most servile and otherwise objectionable class of immigrant' (*Evening Post*, December 1878). The government responded with the Chinese Immigration Act of 1882, which levied a £10 tax on each Chinese who landed in the country and prohibited ships' captains from disembarking more than one Chinese per ten tons of freight. The law was brought in when the Chinese population of New Zealand scarcely numbered 4,500.

In Wellington the Chinese involvement in greengrocery was seen as monopolistic. There were suggestions

Rich and Poor

(reported in the *Evening Post*, June 1889) that the Chinese should live only in specially designated areas of the city. More bitter was an attack published in *Fair Play* in December 1893: 'John, who herds in filthy disease-haunted hovels, is selling cabbages to wealthy Wellingtonians and everyone patronises him — because he is *cheap*.' Anti-Chinese leagues were formed and suggested total bans, raising the entry tax to £100 (which was done in 1896) and called for a prohibition of intermarriage. By the turn of the century there were twelve market gardens around Wellington and fifty-four fruit shops run by the Chinese.

Te Aro flat was the Chinese quarter of colonial Wellington, particularly the area around Haining Street. From time to time a reporter might go into the area, perhaps tagging along with a council health officer, and write up columns of descriptive prose. Particularly titillating were discoveries of rooms crowded with old people, thick with strange-smelling smoke, littered with rotten vegetables, piled high with vegetable crates used as furniture, pervaded by foreign cooking smells and plunged into semi-darkness. 'Haining Street in the afternoon,' reported the *Evening Post* as late as December 1904, 'is conducive to a fit of melancholia. It consists, in brief, of two rows of cottages for the most part miserably unsanitary, dark and dirty, and frequented by listless and unclean Chinese.'

Poverty in Wellington made its most dramatic debut during the 1870s, but this is not to say it ceased to exist later. The relief of poverty is very much part of the story of Wellington. With no universal state aid, much of the onus of relief lay in the hands of private, church and trustee agencies. They attempted to provide money, food, jobs, board, admission to institutions and sometimes travel. These agencies were enormously effective. However, many people never received assistance, possibly because they were loath to apply for it.

Perhaps the best-known charitable agency in Wellington was the Benevolent Trustees, who received money from public donation and the government, and distributed it as best they thought fit. For many years the chairman of the trustees was the city's Rabbi, Herman Van Staveren, one of those larger-than-life figures. Each week the trustees met to listen to cases of hardship. They were also involved with some long-term projects, such as a home for the aged needy, a sector of the population not necessarily catered for by the public hospitals or the asylums. Many of these aged needy had been the strong young pioneers of the early days, but had never had the opportunity to make provision for their old age. A large number of them were also bachelors and thus had no family to lean on. (In those days there were cases of people charged with being neglectful of their parents.)

Wellington was well supplied with institutions and homes for the unfortunate, including such establishments as St Joseph's Orphanage in Hawkestone Street (opened in 1872); Mt View Asylum in Newtown (1874); the Home for Friendless Women in Newtown (1882); the Salvation Army Rescue Home in Majoribanks Street (1886); the Benevolent Trustees Convalescent Home in Ohiro Road (1892); the Indigent Old Men's Home (1892); the Levin Home for Friendless Children in

Berhampore (1895); the Salvation Army Maternity Home for Unmarried Mothers in Ellice Street (1900); and St Joseph's Home for Incurables in Buckle Street (1900).

Another form of relief somewhat different to churches and organisations was the soliciting of public donations by the press. Such donations were most often for specific and usually horrifying misfortunes. It must have been warming to see the degree of response attained. For example, a donation list opened in 1871 for a woman and her six children who had lost their father in a boating accident; it raised £80, which was equivalent to about two years' wages as a harbour worker.

Donations were also made in the form of goods. Among the many published examples of this was when the ship *England* arrived in Wellington in 1872 with a passenger list of Scandinavian immigrants, among whom smallpox had been found. The passengers were diverted to Somes Island, where they were put in quarantine and all their belongings were burned. Through the notice of the press, the people of Wellington flocked to donate everything from money and furniture to reading materials, the acknowledgment of which was nothing short of grateful.

All this relief was beneficial for the immediate demands wrought by poverty. However, the best panacea was a return to a buoyant economy. Even when the country's economy did pick up, poverty remained to some extent. During the first years of the new century when suburbs were filling up with pleasant villas, and new industries were being established, slums still disfigured the centre of the city around Te Aro flat.

Sporadic investigative reports in the press kept these slums in the public mind, and their very existence kept them in the public eye.

WELLINGTON, like most other main centres, has had numerous waves of rebuilding and redevelopment over the decades. By the 1860s few of the buildings from the 1840s were left, and around the turn of the century many of the wooden structures of the 1860s had been replaced by new brick buildings.

Sporadic building in the 1920s gave the city another taste of redevelopment, but it wasn't until the early 1960s that the central cityscape — which had been fairly static since the First World War — started to undergo a redevelopment whose momentum has straddled three decades.

Redevelopment seems to be unavoidable, especially when one takes into account the numerous factors that precipitate it: destruction by fire, decay, increasing land prices, the desire for upgrading, and the potential income from owning property for lease or rental.

A common feature of most cities has been the continuous presence of a number of pioneer commercial concerns through numerous rebuildings. James Smith's Te Aro House started in a shack, was rebuilt in 1868, was burned down and rebuilt in 1885, and today exists on the corner of Manners and Cuba Streets in a large building that was built in 1905 (although admittedly not for James Smith but for ironmonger George Winder) and remodelled in the 1930s to its present Art Deco appearance. Another such example is the National

Bank, whose first premises in Grey Street were built in 1874, rebuilt in 1905, again in 1928 and most recently in 1960.

Many of the city's financial, social and recreational institutions that originated in the pioneering years are still strongly represented in present-day Wellington, albeit in newer buildings with perhaps a different emphasis than before. For example, the rise and expansion of public health facilities from the 'Colonial Hospital' in Thorndon to the sprawling, specialised centre in Newtown reflects the growth of the city and the advances in technology. This development is also echoed in a variety of other institutions as diverse as banking, insurance, education and public edification.

Topographically, Wellington still retains many of the features that both surprised and irritated its settlers, even if the foreshore has been pushed back by a series of time-consuming reclamations, a motorway has eviscerated a ribbon of once domestic 'zoning', and street widening and betterment have removed a fair handful of narrow lanes and rights-of-way. Among the many legacies of the city's topography (and the settlers' reaction to it) are the town plan, and the appearance of the inner suburbs.

The town plan, with its 1100-odd saleable acres and its (latterly criticised) provision for reserves and public spaces, was set on paper long before physical delineation and construction began. Today, many of the original features remain: the generous town belt, major streets like Lambton Quay, the Terrace, Tinakori Road, Cuba Street, Oriental Parade and 'the Adelaide Road' from Courtenay Place to Newtown.

The challenge of topography has produced in a variety of intriguing results in the inner suburbs. Among these are the Kelburn Cable Car, the Karori tunnel, and various cuttings and gradients orginally designed with trams in mind; steep, curved, dead-end and pedestrian-only streets; and a gazetteer of street names perpetuating everything from land owners' names to famous battles.

Indeed, there is much in modern Wellington that has its roots in colonial times. This of course gives rise to an ongoing debate about what to preserve and what to let go. Destructive fires have removed a surprising number of fine buildings from Wellington, and redevelopment occasioned by obsolescence (or sheer greed) goes on. Although the city has lost a number of very fine gems, others remain which should have the benefit of preservation.

To be transfixed by the future without an occasional glance back at the past scarcely qualifies as progress, and certainly not as foresight.

ILLUSTRATIONS

The small scale and occasional elegant nature of the commercial buildings on Lambton Quay can be seen in this photograph, taken in 1868. The second building from the left (built in 1864) was one of the many ironmongery warehouses of Edward Mills whose *leitmotif* was a cast-iron sculpture of a British Lion. Mills lived not so far away at 'Sayes Court', an imposing house on Aurora Terrace which later disappeared (along with most of its subsoil) in the motorway construction. In 1879 Mills transferred his Lambton Quay store, and the British Lion, further along the Quay. 'Owing to his Highness' weight some little difficulty was experienced in getting him onto the position he occupies, and where it is presumed he will calmly be monarch of all he surveys,' reported the *New Zealand Mail* in November 1881.

Mills's new building was originally constructed for well-known colonial merchant Lipman Levy, whose own private estate in Mt Victoria was soon to be subdivided with access from Lipman and Levy Streets.

On the skyline can be seen a rather tentatively fenced stretch of Wellington Terrace, and in the foreground, work is proceeding on building the breastwork necessary to reclaim land from the harbour.

WELLINGTON PUBLIC LIBRARY

This view of lower Willis Street further illustrates the appearance of commercial Wellington in the 1860s. At the time Willis Street was almost as important as Lambton Quay. In the mid-1890s it was almost fully redeveloped as a thoroughfare of brick premises. This photo shows the rough nature of the buildings. There were few regulations covering construction, resulting in a prevalence of lean-tos and narrow alleys, and the encroachment of buildings onto the street. The problem of encroachment alarmed the City Council so much that it commissioned a surveyor, Thomas Ward, to produce a map showing the limits of every single building in Wellington. It was an enormous exercise in cartography. Completed in 1891, the map was used to enforce the demolition of encroaching buildings, to codify street lines and provide data for street-widening purposes. Willis Street started to be widened in the 1890s. All the buildings on the left-hand side of this photograph were gradually removed, a procedure that involved the Council in several claims for compensation. The photograph was taken in fine weather and understates the rough conditions of the road, which could become impassable in the wet.

WELLINGTON PUBLIC LIBRARY

This harbour-side view of Lambton Quay taken c. 1870 shows the first line-up of new buildings, all designed by Christian Toxward, on the recently reclaimed land. On the left is the emporium of Joseph Burne, an early settler who, like many others, consolidated his wealth with property investments. He lived not far away on the Terrace. In the middle is Toxward's own office with its delicate facade decoration. Toxward was among the first of Wellington's architects and his design skill and public profile led him to produce a number of commercial, religious and domestic buildings.

On the right are the premises of Charles Barraud, chemist and artist. Barraud arranged the ground floor of this building as a shop and dispensary and used the upper floor as an art gallery. The two front windows of the gallery contained stained-glass depictions of the muse Poetry, executed by Lavers and Barraud of London. On the street facade flanking the upper-floor windows were niches for two statues, one depicting Medicine and one Art. A statue of a phoenix was later placed on top of the building's pediment. Little wonder the *Evening Post* described the building as 'one of the most tasty erections in this city' on its opening in October 1868. The site of these three buildings now forms part of the Harbour City Centre.
DENTON COLLECTION. ALEXANDER TURNBULL LIBRARY

OPPOSITE

The style and scale of commercial premises of the 1870s is aptly illustrated in this view of the northern end of Lambton Quay — finely modelled double-storeyed premises with large show windows and some intricately carved detail. On the far right is Mrs Hill's registry office — an early form of labour exchange — built in the 1850s. Next to this are the double premises of Mrs Cowles, toyseller, and Cook and Son, tailors. The building was designed in 1870 by Christian Toxward. Next door is one of the tiny infill building which typified many of New Zealand's shopping streets at the time. This one is occupied by Price the hairdresser. To the left of this is the formal-looking grocery shop of Houston Logan, designed in 1874 by Charles Tringham. Across the narrow alley and cut in half by the limit of the camera plate is Steele's drapery, designed in 1874 by Christian Toxward. Seemingly presiding over the proceedings in the near background is Government House, the residence of the colony's English-appointed Governor. All the buildings on this section of the Quay were demolished to make way for the War Memorial Cenotaph and the realignment of Bowen Street in the late 1920s.
ALEXANDER TURNBULL LIBRARY

GOVERNMENT HOUSE
WELLINGTON

55

This view of the intersection of Willis and Manners Street illustrates some of the typical wooden buildings that were erected in the 1870s. They achieved a greater height, scale and degree of decoration than the smaller, starker buildings of the 1860s. On the corner, now referred to as Perrett's Corner, is the fifteen-roomed house and surgery designed for Dr Harding by Thomas Turnbull in 1878. Many a combined house and surgery was built in the area around Willis Street, which was popular among doctors and dentists. In Dr Harding's house the private rooms, including a schoolroom, were on the upper floor. The surgery was on the ground floor, and the basement, formed by the sloping site, contained the kitchen and servants' quarters. This building was much disfigured over the years and was finally demolished in the early 1970s. Next to Dr Harding's residence along Manners Street are the three-storeyed premises of Beck and Tonks, general merchants, designed in 1876 by Charles Tringham. Its smart facade and contrastingly plain side walls were typical of the buildings of the time.

ALEXANDER TURNBULL LIBRARY

The premises of Jacob Joseph on Lambton Quay dramatically show both the scale and solidity achieved by brick particularly when contrasted with the small wooden buildings erected barely a decade earlier. On its completion this building achieved the status of a landmark, not just because of its pioneering construction and height, but also because it impaired the harbour view from the Wellington Club on the Terrace behind. Joseph had been refused membership to the club and decided to interfere with its view — an ironic course of action as Joseph himself was blind.

The construction of this block was observed with some interest. However, there were complaints about the encroachment of scaffolding on to the footpath, forcing pedestrians to use the muddy road. A lawsuit was also threatened by a passing carriage of well-dressed ladies when falling lime burnt holes in their costumes.

This building was completed in 1878. The ground floor was used for wine and spirits, the three middle floors for drapery and the top floor for ironmongery. Two lifts serviced the building, one powered by steam for heavy loads, and the other powered manually. In 1883 the building was taken over by Harcourts, and subsequent owners have included the Wairarapa Farmers Co-op, Kempthorne Prosser, and Coulls, Sommerville and Wilkie. The site is now occupied by Lambton Square.

ELLIS COLLECTION. ALEXANDER TURNBULL LIBRARY

OPPOSITE

James Smith's Te Aro House in Cuba Street was designed by Thomas Turnbull in 1885 to replace premises damaged by fire. Mindful of fire safety, Turnbull specified an all-brick structure, including internal walls, to contain fire if it broke out. A series of perforated pipes along the roof acted as an early form of sprinkler system, although this was never required to be used. The facade to Cuba Street was decorated with window trim and parapet detail, lending it an air of attractiveness and self-assurance, appropriate for a commercial building. Its verandah with cast-iron trim and heraldic devices gave the building visual prominence in a street of otherwise plain premises. Also notable was the observation tower built in wood. Such was the excitement of the new building that James Smith hired fifty boys to act as sandwich-board carriers to parade through town on Saturday nights between 6 and 8 p.m.

TYREE COLLECTION, ALEXANDER TURNBULL LIBRARY

In 1868 Christian Toxward designed new premises for the well-established drapers, Kirkcaldie and Stains. It was the first building to be erected on this reclaimed block of land. A new Kirkcaldie and Stains building, still standing today, was later constructed on the same site. The building shown was the second premises of the drapers on the quay. Their first, Waterloo House, was a long wooden block on the site now occupied by the old Bank of New Zealand. Toxward's building was acclaimed by the press on its opening, not only for its elegant appearance, but also for its use of local wood for internal fittings, and vast plate glass windows set in cedar frames. Toxward's building was auctioned for removal in 1908 to allow part of the present building to go up.

NATIONAL MUSEUM, WELLINGTON, NEG. B 9762

The growth of Kirkcaldie and Stains from a single wooden building to an entire block's frontage of Lambton Quay was steady and well planned. In this view, the ornate middle block was designed by Thomas Turnbull in 1897. It was built on the site of Reichardt's piano warehouse, and the salvaged wood from Reichardt's premises was used by John Kirkcaldie to build a seaside house at Plimmerton. At the same time, Kirkcaldie also greatly added to his own private residence 'Kinnoul' on Thompson Street, and on its completion treated his retail staff to a garden party there. This middle block used steel girders and foundation stones imported from Australia, which delayed completion, and inside was sited the famous tearooms, separated from the shop by an arcade of Gothic arches.

In 1908, William Turnbull (Thomas's son) designed the two wings flanking the middle block, and in 1928 the middle block was shorn of its finery and remodelled to fit in with the new wings.

Site redevelopment has recently produced two tower blocks (designed by Morrison, Cooper and partners) fitted behind the retained and strengthened facade of 1908.

WELLINGTON PUBLIC LIBRARY

This row of imposing buildings on Lambton Quay typifies the solidity and commercial flavour of the years around the turn of the century. Built in reinforced brick covered with plaster, the buildings drew their decorative features from a wide range of historical styles, which *in toto* produced an overwhelmingly busy but majestic appearance.

On the right is the building designed in 1901 by William Chatfield for the *New Zealand Times* and *New Zealand Mail* newspapers, with the printing house extending behind almost the full length of Cable Car Lane. In the middle is the Star Chambers, designed in 1902 by William Chatfield for E. C. Batkin, a local tobacconist whose keen involvement with the Star Boating Club led him to name his building after it. On the left is the building designed in 1903 by John Swan for Gamble and Creed.

These buildings, all demolished in 1980 to make way for the Phoenix Centre, were built to generate income, hence the number of floors and offices for letting.

WELLINGTON CITY COUNCIL COLLECTION, ALEXANDER TURNBULL LIBRARY

another floor — hence the two rows of cornices at the top — thus requiring a further order of steel joists from Australia. One of the flags submitted for the Australian Federal Flag competition carrying emblems representing Australia's six states was hoisted on top of the building on its opening. The King's Chambers were demolished to make way for the BNZ head office.
ALEXANDER TURNBULL LIBRARY

OPPOSITE

This glimpse of a rather empty Panama Street, taken about 1879 by a visiting Nelson photographer, captures the architectural panache of some of the town's warehouses. On the far left, cut in half by the limit of the camera plate, is the auction house of R. J. Duncan, built in 1873 on the corner of Panama Street and Lambton Quay. Next door is the new building of R. J. Duncan, designed in 1876 by Charles Tringham in a style echoing Italian commercial architecture. This building was bought in 1879 by Thomas Kennedy Macdonald and became widely known as Macdonald's Building. The flag hanging from the first-floor window is advertising one of the many regular auctions of goods as diverse as real estate and unredeemed items from pawnshops. Next to Macdonald's Building is the warehouse of Thompson, Shannon, softgoods dealers, designed in 1875 by Charles Tringham. Across a small vacant section is the warehouse of Johnston and Co., also designed by Tringham in 1873.

In 1887 a spectacular fire destroyed the first three buildings. The Johnston warehouse escaped only because it was protected by a brick warehouse which had been erected in the vacant section. Panama Street was one of the first new streets on the reclaimed land fronting Lambton Quay. It was named after the Panama Canal, which had recently opened, greatly reducing shipping time between New Zealand and England.
ALEXANDER TURNBULL LIBRARY

The King's Chambers were so called to honour the first new monarch in the city's history. This photograph was taken shortly after the building was completed in February 1904. Its size and appearance provide an indication of its contemporary status. Designed by William Chatfield, the building required half a million bricks and cost £30,000 to erect. After a year of construction, it was decided to add

ABOVE

This photograph, taken about 1870, shows the intersection of Lambton Quay with Featherston Street. The warehouse in the middle was designed in 1868 by Benjamin Smith for merchant William Bannatyne. Although fairly severe in appearance the building is not without touches of decoration. Its warehouse function is plainly evident by the number of large cart entrances on the ground floor. The building was removed in 1908 and a new structure called Baker's Building was designed by Penty and Blake for the Bannatyne estate on the same site. It was replaced by the present AMP Chambers in 1951.

Across a fenced section along Featherston Street stands one of the many warehouses of Edward Mills, ironmonger and foundry owner. This building with its pretty facade was erected in 1867 for land investor John Martin and was also designed by Benjamin Smith. Mills's magnificent iron statue of a lion can clearly be seen on the pediment — his foundry was called the Lion Foundry. A few years after this photo was taken, Mills had larger premises built next door and the small building of 1867 became known as Temple Chambers, housing a number of law firms until its destruction by fire in 1901.

Across Grey Street to the left can be seen another group of ironmongery warehouses belonging originally to William Gibson and removed in 1908 to make way for the vast extensions to the city's Chief Post Office.

ALEXANDER TURNBULL LIBRARY

LEFT

In 1873 Christian Toxward designed this warehouse for Joseph Nathan on the corner of Featherston and Grey Streets at a cost of £4,000. It was the city's tallest building and contained the city's first hydraulic lift. Its interior space was filled with ironmongery, drapery and fancy goods. A reporter who went along to view the place on its opening was particularly fascinated by the drapery on the second floor: 'in one part of the room there are unmentionables enough to supply an army; and in another direction there is a cloud of ostrich feathers' (*New Zealand Mail*, May 1874).

In 1881 the building had all its ceilings and the roof laid with perforated water pipes as a form of sprinkler system. The press found this intriguing and sensible, yet it proved ineffective in 1902 when a fire destroyed much of the building. However, the wood that was salvaged (mainly totara and red pine) was good enough to be reused, and much of it was bought by cabinet-makers who turned it into furniture.

Shortly after the fire, Joshua Charlesworth designed a magnificent seven-storeyed replacement. This new Nathan's Building was a prominent landmark in Featherston Street until its demolition in the mid-1970s.

AUTHOR

RIGHT

One of the original lessees of the newly reclaimed land along Customhouse Quay was the general merchant firm W. and G. Turnbull. In 1877 they commissioned Thomas Turnbull to design a substantial warehouse for the site. Turnbull's design was severe in appearance and it was only the slight arching of the windows that lent it any visual softness. Yet it was the building's scale and its construction in unplastered brick that gave the name Turnbull (*both* merchant and architect) some public prominence. The photograph, taken during construction, shows the two side blocks of the warehouse which were joined by a four-storeyed central block in 1886. As a warehouse it provided a vast area for goods storage and provided a visual demarcation between land and sea from the harbour.

The Turnbull warehouse was put to numerous uses over the years and was finally demolished to make way for BP House.

AUTHOR

65

ROSLYN

P. HAYMAN & Co.

1890

EMPIRE HOTEL

OPPOSITE

This view of a rather busy Victoria Street, taken about 1916, displays the elaborate facades deemed appropriate in the golden age of merchant warehouse building. At the right of this view (and partially cut off) is the warehouse of the Dunedin-based merchants Bing, Harris. It was designed in 1890 by Thomas Turnbull but tripled in length in 1898 by William Chatfield.

Next door is the Victoria Street entrance of the Empire Hotel, a luxury establishment which went through to Willis Street. It was built in 1897 to designs by George Schwartz, who was treated by the hotel's owner, Joseph Mandel, to a study tour of Australia prior to building to gather the latest ideas in luxuries and appointments. The hotel was suitably well patronised, and an extension of fifty rooms was added to the top of the building in 1904.

To the left of the Empire is one of the first warehouses for Hayman and Co., designed in 1887 by William Chatfield. Such was the expansion of this firm that Chatfield was called on to design a new building for the firm in 1905 on the neighbouring section. This six-storeyed building is also shown and was the tallest structure in Wellington at the time. It cost £20,000 to build, and its floors were entirely given over to the company's imports which included stationery, tobacco, jewellery, cutlery, toys, furnishings, drugs and crockery, and which required the services of three electric lifts.

None of the buildings in this photo still stands.

HALSE COLLECTION, ALEXANDER TURNBULL LIBRARY

In 1870 the Colonial Architect William Clayton, whose conditions of employment allowed him to accept private jobs, designed this butcher's shop for James Gear on Lambton Quay. With its painted 'marbled' effect to the ground floor walls, its enormous display windows, and interior fittings arranged in a large horse-shoe shape, it brought the name Gear into prominence. The shop was opened in a rather grand manner with a special display of meat from the Wairarapa 'embracing 40 sheep, 6 bullocks, 4 calves and 4 pigs'. Further assisting Gear Meat's rise to industrial stardom was the building of a factory behind this shop in 1882 to cope with the demand resulting from the company's diversification into canned and preserved meat. Preserving had started in 1873 and even then, with a production of 800 tins a day, local demand was such that it precluded export until a larger operation came into being.

Clayton's wooden building was removed in 1898 to make way for a larger building whose upper floor had living quarters for the company's bachelor employees as well as a suite of rooms for the manager and his family.

TYREE COLLECTION, ALEXANDER TURNBULL LIBRARY

This appetising view is the interior of James Gear's butchery on Lambton Quay. The building went up in 1870 and was soon followed by a preserving factory behind it, and a branch establishment in Cuba Street.

The city's butchers worked extremely long hours before agitation and legislation changed their working conditions. Up to the 1880s their week consisted of over eighty hours, and included all-day Saturday shopping which dragged on past 10 p.m. Grocers and drapers also stayed open late on Saturdays and until 7 p.m. during the week until protest altered conditions. Much of the protest came from the Early Closing Movement, a vigilante group that forced a widespread early closing of shops with various success and by various means. Somewhat embarrassing, and calculated to bring onlookers, was their method of holding speeches and playing instruments outside offending shops. In one instance in September 1884 they were fined over £3 for breaching the peace.

By the early 1890s, the pattern of shops shutting at 6 p.m. at nights was well in place, and had been codified by law as the Shop Hours Bill.

ALEXANDER TURNBULL LIBRARY

Another burgeoning colonial industry, particularly towards the 1890s, was furniture-making, and almost every town of reasonable size had at least one such factory and showroom. Locally made furniture, while following overseas trends in style, could be of high quality, and the country's forests yielded much of the timber necessary. Further helping the trade was a widespread insistence on local furnishings for large projects like government departments, schools, churches, hotels and tourists resorts.

This photo shows the well-known Scoullar and Chisholm showroom on Lambton Quay, a mere vacant section away from the Gear Meat premises. The building was designed in 1889 by William Chatfield, built for £4,000, and on its opening, was seen as standing 'like a giant amongst pigmies, and will probably set the fashion for a substantial class of business places when rebuilding in the neighbourhood fairly sets in' (*Evening Post*, January 1890).

Standing in front of the building is a horse-drawn dray with the firm's name on the side. Any self-respecting retailing concern used such effective methods of advertising to keep their name in the public mind.

TYREE COLLECTION, ALEXANDER TURNBULL LIBRARY

Off Manners Street runs a narrow lane called Luke's Lane on which once stood the extensive iron foundry of Luke and Son. It was one of a number of foundries in Wellington which turned out a range of ironware for domestic and commercial use, steam boilers, small vessels and cranes. (Other major foundries include those owned by E. W. Mills, William Cable, Edward Seager and William Dawson.) Luke's premises occupied over half a hectare of land and when busy, might employ up to 150 people, some of whom have posed for this photograph.

Industries like foundries, and other concerns like warehousing, the railways, building construction and shipping, were substantial employers in colonial Wellington. The work was arduous, predominantly manual, had little security of tenure and was not lavishly rewarded.

MARITIME MUSEUM COLLECTION, ALEXANDER TURNBULL LIBRARY

OPPOSITE

An entire block is taken up by the ironmongery warehouses of William Dawson in this view of Featherston Street. Half the buildings are sheathed in corrugated iron, a rather humorous way of advertising their wares. Ironmongery was a lucrative business, as iron was the dominant roofing material in Wellington.

The photograph also shows the metalling of the street. Many attempts were made to get the streets into fair condition, and the shingle was taken, without charge, from the Hutt River and sold to the City Council by astute contractors. The shingling of the streets, done on a large scale in the late 1870s, offered relief work for the unemployed who undertook physically to break it down into an agreed grade — work that paid 7s a day, about the average rate for a labourer.

The horses in the photograph are a reminder of the dominant method of hauling and transport for those wealthy enough to afford it. Sometimes the horses would 'bolt' when frightened, and suddenly gallop along streets causing havoc and often injury. Sadly, the mistreatment of horses made the SPCA one of the more vigorous public societies to be established in colonial Wellington.

NATIONAL MUSEUM, WELLINGTON, NEG. B 15595

71

The Union Bank of Australia premises in this photograph display the grand, albeit small-scaled, architectural panache lent to a building of important function. It was constructed in 1852 when the corner of Willis and Boulcott Streets was strategically near the centre of the business district. Attached to the banking chamber is the manager's house — the provision of accommodation was standard practice throughout the country as the frequent transfers of managers from branch to branch was an established feature of banking.

The view shows the poor condition of the city's roads before serious attempts at surfacing were made, and indeed before footpaths were formed and a system of stormwater drains established. The denuded hills behind have been sown in grass, and the few lines of fencing suggest their use as grazing paddocks. Grazing so close to town was used more for horses than for sheep — the sheep-farming area of the province at this time was the Wairarapa.

In 1877 this building was put up for auction and bought by John Plimmer for £1,600. Plimmer designed for the site an intriguing hotel called the Albert, but more commonly known as the Old Identities. The site is now occupied by the St George Hotel.

ALEXANDER TURNBULL LIBRARY

Many of the banks built premises in the heart of the commercial centre on Lambton Quay, and demanded their architects produce buildings of immediate distinction and stylistic flair. In 1874 the Union Bank asked Christian Toxward to design new premises for their recently acquired apex section between the Quay and Featherston Street. Toxward's singular building, constructed in wood for £5,500, was an unusual design drawing on Greek stylistic components. Its large central banking chamber had a floor of English tiles and counters made from Sydney cedar — one of the first uses of imported luxury materials in the city.

In front of the fenced garden can be seen the drinking fountain presented to Wellington by well-heeled farmer, investor and politician John Martin. It was unveiled in June 1876, although the lights ordered from overseas had been twice broken in transit and a third set had not yet arrived. After the official opening a hundred invited guests withdrew to the nearby Empire Hotel for luncheon. One of the toasts expressed the hope that gifts from citizens who had become wealthy through the city might prove contagious.

All the buildings in this photo were destroyed by fire: the Union Bank in 1906, and those along Featherston Street in 1907 (the three-storeyed Mills warehouse at the right) and 1902 (the two buildings to the left of the Mills building).

ALEXANDER TURNBULL LIBRARY

OPPOSITE

The apex site between Lambton and Customhouse Quays gave the Bank of New Zealand a visual prominence. The nucleus of the building was designed in 1863 by Mason and Ross of Dunedin. Looking convincingly as if constructed in stone, the building was in fact made of wood. This view shows the finished building with extensions designed by Thomas Turnbull in 1877. The extensions were so finely worked through that it is hard to identify the original building. The use of a bull-nosed corner, side entrance and the slight stepping of the facades made it one of the more interesting and subtly modelled banking premises in the country. In 1898 the building was sold for £50 and removed to allow redevelopment of the site.

Further along Customhouse Quay to the right are two more wooden financial buildings — the decorated AMP premises, and next to it, the Bank of Australasia. Both were designed by Christian Toxward, and both have long since been demolished.

AUTHOR

The BNZ head office was designed by Thomas Turnbull in a grand, decorated style which spoke of solidity and dependability. Turnbull was asked to design the premises after he had won a competition for a building proposed for a different site. However, the finished construction differed from Turnbull's drawn design by omitting three corner towers, thus reducing the height from four to three floors and shearing away much wall ornamentation. These amendments were made because the tenders received were too high — somewhere in the order of £15,000 above the architect's estimates. Fresh tenders were sought for the revised plans; eleven were received and the successful contractor — Carmichael and Son with a price of £22,500 — started work within hours of securing the job. Construction went smoothly and towards opening day the public was invited to view the boardroom furniture on display at Fielders showroom in Manners Street. This furniture had been made from the timber of 'Noah's Ark', a beached ship once standing on the site that was used as a warehouse and auction rooms.

BNZ ARCHIVES

In 1874 Christian Toxward designed this building with its elaborate street front for the National Bank in Grey Street. Modelled in wood and lavished with Toxward's love of ornament, it was built back slightly from the footpath, allowing Toxward to give it a smart iron fence which helped to set it apart from its plainer neighbours. In 1906 the building was auctioned as salvaged timber, the auction notice mentioning how the totara capitals would be suitable for 'garden, flower or fern stands'.

Its replacement was a brick building designed by John Swan, which was replaced by a larger building in 1928. This has also been replaced by the present bank building.

WELLINGTON PUBLIC LIBRARY

OPPOSITE

One of the more imposing Edwardian buildings on Lambton Quay was the Bank of New South Wales, pictured here in the last stages of construction in mid-1905. It was designed by Crichton and McKay and built by an Australian firm for £35,000. It was a large and expensive undertaking. The construction work was supervised by the City Council to ensure as little public disruption as possible. This supervision was needed because a lot of building was underway in the city at the time, and the main streets were being dug up to lay electric tram lines and then wood-blocked for heavy traffic. Within months of its completion the building was gutted in the extensive fire of 1906, the fire spreading into the building through open side windows. The building was reinstated, its roof designed to be flooded in the event of another fire and all the windows fitted with iron shutters to be closed at night. Reinstatement cost £27,500. It was demolished in 1972 and the site is now occupied by the Westpac tower.

To the right of the bank can be seen the Italian Renaissance-styled building designed in 1896 by Thomas Turnbull for booksellers Whitcombe and Tombs. This finely modelled building, costing £6,000, was also severely damaged in the 1906 fire, and was replaced by the present premises designed by William Turnbull.

ALEXANDER TURNBULL LIBRARY

OPPOSITE

Perhaps the finest Classically modelled wooden building in the country was the AMP premises on the corner of Featherston and Hunter Streets, designed in 1877 by Christian Toxward. Toxward extended his standard decoration with a florid frieze at first floor level and a wealth of cornice and parapet detail to hide the plain slate roof.

Within two decades Toxward's building became too small for its purpose and was replaced in 1897 by a larger building designed along almost exactly the same stylistic lines but built in brick. The new building was the work of Frederick Clere (Toxward had died in 1891), an architect who was better known for his numerous churches than his commercial work. Clere's building also lasted only a few decades. It was replaced in 1927 by the present AMP building, which was designed by Frederick's son, Edmund Clere.

AMP SOCIETY

One of the giants of insurance in the country was the Auckland-based New Zealand Insurance Company whose meteoric rise as a financial institution was paralleled by that of the Bank of New Zealand. This photograph shows the Wellington branch of NZI on the corner of Lambton Quay and Grey Street. The building had been constructed for local merchant firm Edmondson and Sellars in 1872 to designs by Christian Toxward but was taken over by NZI four years later and refitted by Thomas Turnbull. Much of Turnbull's work was in the interior fittings which were 'composed of tastily arranged and fantastically-carved New Zealand woods' (*New Zealand Mail*, November 1876). Turnbull was also responsible for a massive glass screen in the vestibule, decorated with illuminated writing in blue, red and gold, with emblems, scrollwork and native flora as a background.

Attached to the Grey Street wall on the left of the premises can be seen one of many fire ladders put in prominent places in 1878 for fire rescue. Painted a brilliant red and supplied with a placard explaining their use, they were common features in most major cities at the time.

In 1906 fire destroyed this building and its entire block. It was replaced by a brick building designed by Penty and Blake. Today the ANZ tower covers the entire block.

ALEXANDER TURNBULL LIBRARY

OPPOSITE

The first insurance company to build brick premises in Wellington was the National Mutual group, which commissioned Thomas Turnbull to design this imposing building for them in 1884. It cost an astonishing £25,000 to build. It was the plasterwork that set the building apart from most of the city's other brick structures. The plasterwork detail included carved heads with twisted mouths at the top of the ground floor arches and was carried through into interior details like door surrounds, ceilings and stairwells.

The building went up on reclaimed land, and, more particularly, on the site of 'Noah's Ark', the beached vessel which had been turned into a warehouse. Unfortunately, when reclamation was done, much of 'Noah's Ark' was not removed, and the trapped stagnant water soon gave rise to a fearful stench in some of the building's rented offices. A round of law suits was threatened, and medical opinion was sought about the danger of this water. Wellington was known for its high death rate due to infectious diseases spread through bacteria in stagnant water.

The BNZ head office was later built alongside the National Mutual premises. This building is the finest piece of Thomas Turnbull's elaborate architectural design still standing.

ALEXANDER TURNBULL LIBRARY

The CML building on Customhouse Quay, designed in 1896 by William Chatfield, illustrated the pomp of the late-colonial style at its extreme. This was the stylistic generation between the delicacy of earlier wooden buildings and the strong, sparsely decorated office blocks a few decades later.

This building was demolished in 1933 for new premises, which were in turn replaced by the recently constructed CML tower. Such extensive site redevelopment is typical of almost every central business street in Wellington — more so than in any other city in the country.

Customhouse Quay was the insurance golden mile of Wellington, and CML shared its premises with the Phoenix Insurance Company. Just visible to the left of CML is William Turnbull's 1903 building for the Australian Widows' Fund Life Association, which cost £11,000 and was faced with Pyrmont stone imported from Sydney.

CML

Despite the damage to the negative, this photograph, taken in the mid-1860s, provides a good idea of the importance and state of the waterfront. The area is now Jervois Quay. Full reclamation of the land was not complete until about thirty years after this photograph was taken. Many harbourside sites were occupied by boat-building yards (see central foreground), sailmakers and coal yards. The boat yards, often small family businesses, could turn out a surprising range of boats, racing canoes and yachts, although they were no match for the handful of large engineering works producing passenger steamers, freighters and coal hulks.

The waterfront was also often used as a giant rubbish dump. Littering was loudly criticised, but it was not until the Council expended heavily on drainage, rubbish collection and a public destructor that the volume of litter in the harbour, and the incidence of infectious diseases, were reduced.

ALEXANDER TURNBULL LIBRARY

One of the landmarks of pioneer Wellington was John Plimmer's 'Noah's Ark'. This was the wreck of the *Inconstant*, a ship that set off from Adelaide but struck rocks at the Wellington heads in 1849. It was too damaged to restore and so Plimmer bought it for £80 and had it towed to the Quay, a voyage which took five days because of rough weather. When it had settled on its new site, Plimmer removed its upper work and built a two-storeyed warehouse and auction rooms onto it, which opened in mid-1851, and which was reached by a short causeway. The earthquake of 1855 threw the whole establishment onto its side and after being righted it was packed with earth and provided a new piece of land valued at £450. This photo shows the 'ark' being dismantled in 1884.

ALEXANDER TURNBULL LIBRARY

This view of Queen's Wharf, taken about 1867, shows its multiple moorings and numerous crossbars. Built by the Provincial Government and later taken over by the Wellington Harbour Board, it was the city's major public wharf. This photograph was taken before large sheds were built in 1872 and shows the wharf completely free of goods. To the right is the cluster of buildings erected in 1862 for the Post and Telegraph Department — buildings that had to suffice for well over twenty years until a new post office was constructed. In the foreground work is being carried out around what is now Panama Street. The muddy and arduous nature of this work is clearly evident. The railway tracks used for conveying trucks of spoil to the site can also be seen.

ALEXANDER TURNBULL LIBRARY

OPPOSITE

This tranquil photograph of the waterfront somewhat belies its usually bustling condition. The long wharves reaching out to deep-water moorings are a dominant feature of the area. In the central background is Queen's Wharf, with one of many large storage sheds built along it, thus reducing the congestion caused by unloading vessels. The large iron building on the left is the Queen's Bond where customs duty (a revenue earner for the government) was levied and collected from incoming goods. This building served until 1890 when it was replaced with the much finer looking Queen's Bond and Harbour Board Office.

Just below the bondstore can be seen a slip where watermen running a freight taxi service launched their boats. This slip was known as the 'gridiron'. The watermen were indispensable around the harbour. They often ventured out in rough weather, which meant accidents and drownings were not unknown.

TYREE COLLECTION, ALEXANDER TURNBULL LIBRARY

85

OPPOSITE

This view towards Lambton Quay shows the 1866 reclamation of about five hectares well underway. In 1878 a further reclamation was completed, providing a total of twenty-four hectares of new land. The area shown here was dubbed 'the city dust heap' when reclamation was finished, and while some people were eager to build on the new land, the City Council had to decide whether to sell or lease it. In the end the Council leased it and would only auction sites if they received more than one tenderer. The land from the 1878 reclamation was divided into sections and sold at an auction in early 1879. The auction raised close to £100,000 and ended with a champagne lunch provided by the auctioneer, R. J. Duncan.

The two buildings prominent on Lambton Quay are the Athenaeum and Mechanics' Institute to the left, and next to it the original Presbyterian Church which, when replaced by a larger building in 1866, was rolled across the street and remodelled as a shop.

ALEXANDER TURNBULL LIBRARY

A trestle railway was erected by the contractors for the Te Aro reclamation to deliver spoil from the quarries around Oriental Bay. Part of it is shown in this photograph, taken in 1884. A number of whales can also be seen on the sand. These were slaughtered by employees of the gas works — an event which drew over 2,000 onlookers and proved quite profitable for the men who killed them. Not only were they able to sell the oil, but they also put the whales on public display at the bottom of Tory Street and charged 1s to see them.

Some children can be seen playing on the railway. Judging by the stern warnings in the local press, the railway was obviously a favourite playground. The trestle railway carried an average of 200 trucks of spoil a day. The engines produced numerous showers of sparks, which understandably alarmed the house owners of Oriental Bay for some years.

ALEXANDER TURNBULL LIBRARY

In 1857 the Wellington Provincial Government bought two acres (about one hectare) and was granted a third as a site for its chambers. A design competition was held, the terms of which betrayed Wellington's ambition to become the capital — the proposed building was called the House of General Assembly. A military engineer, George Single, won the competition and most of the building was completed within the year at a cost of £2,000. Various additions were made to the structure over the next few years, including a library at the rear. Part of Single's building was demolished when the new additions to Parliament went up in the 1870s and the remainder was dismantled in 1898 to clear the site for the General Assembly Library. Built from native pine, Single's building had by this time become so rotten and worm-eaten that although the men employed to build the General Assembly Library were allowed to take the wood home for their own use, few bothered.

ALEXANDER TURNBULL LIBRARY

Clayton's Parliament Buildings were complicated in composition. This photograph, taken in 1872, shows the wealth of curious detail lavished on it. Because of the enormous amount of timber needed for its construction, Clayton advertised tenders throughout New Zealand. However, the contract was won by local timber merchants. Completed by mid-1873, it was lit by gas for the first ten years. In 1883 it was fitted with electricity, providing a brilliant light in contrast with the yellow, dingy appearance of the gas. When the building was finished tenders were advertised for new furniture. However, the prices received were considered too high and a large order was placed in England. In the meantime, the old furniture from the earlier building was installed and was reportedly very shabby.

Fire was always a possibility in a wooden building such as this, and although rubber hoses had been installed from the outset, the structure was totally razed in 1907. The fire already had a firm grip on the building by the time thousands of spectators gathered to watch in the early hours one morning in December.

AUTHOR

The General Assembly Library was built by the government using day labour after tenders received from contractors were deemed too high. Progress on the building was fraught with problems as a result of the day labour scheme. The 2,000,000 bricks needed were manufactured in Wellington, many of them by the prisoners at Mt Cook. Although the building was to cost £40,000, it was never clear whether Parliament had sanctioned the money. The Public Works Department became contractor and paymaster, but a strike interrupted the work because the pay was several shillings per day short, and often arrived late. Some of the workers, particularly those who had come from other cities, had to pawn their belongings to live. Arbitration was resorted to after a second strike, and the *Evening Post* applauded the men for speaking out against a government which seemed to keep 'the majority of its employees in a state of terrorism' (April 1898).

Work progressed smoothly in 1899. A plaster moulding factory was set up in the grounds and plaster workers employed for up to fourteen hours a day. The building survived the 1907 fire reasonably well, and remains one of the city's most admired structures from this period.

AUTHOR

Government House was designed in 1868 by William Clayton, who was living in Dunedin at the time but soon shifted to Wellington. Several expensive tenders were received and construction began the following year after the design was altered to reduce costs — plaster linings were used instead of wood, brick chimneys instead of iron, and gravel paths instead of asphalt. The building contractor was underwritten for £10,600 by local businessman John Martin, who lost out as the total cost, including furnishings, was close to £33,000. The government was slow to pay and it was rumoured that Martin was going to take drastic action to recover costs. The *Evening Post* reported that a guard had been posted 'to prevent Mr Martin taking the house for the damage, and removing it bodily some night' (March 1871). Further discontent arose when Clayton decided to use prison labour to clear and plant out the grounds. It was considered too late as a cost-cutting exercise, and such work, it was felt, should be given to the unemployed of the city.

As a vice-regal residence, Government House was certainly a grand edifice. It contained two drawing rooms, a dining room, a ballroom, billiard room, conservatory, twenty bedrooms and various offices. In 1869 stables for ten horses and a coach house for five carriages were built. With a substantial staff of one butler, four kitchen maids, three housemaids, two ladies' maids and a school maid, the running of the house was in good hands.

E. R. WILLIAMS COLLECTION, ALEXANDER TURNBULL LIBRARY

ABOVE

The Government Buildings on Lambton Quay were built in 1875 by local contractors Archibald and Scoullar, who ran a large fence around the site during construction to prevent people entering. Apart from a strike by plasterers who wanted 12s instead of 11s a day, construction went smoothly and the building was occupied by the end of 1876. The following year the building was surrounded by an ugly wooden fence, which the *Evening Post* thought was a 'remarkably fine specimen of the order of architecture lately in vogue for public buildings in Wellington', and suggested it should be termed the 'coal-shed', or 'calf-pen'. '. . . It will prove useful as well as ornamental, presenting an impassable barrier to any naughty civil servants who desire to play truant during office-hours' (May 1877). The fence was replaced by the present iron railings in 1901.

The Government Buildings were constructed in wood, and fire prevention was taken seriously right from the outset. One precaution was the prohibition of smoking inside the building. Notices to this effect were posted on the walls in both English and Maori. By the mid-1880s water mains had been laid around the building and pipes installed to all four floors. Small fire engines, hose reels and buckets of water were installed. A fire brigade was formed among the workers and every night two watchmen patrolled the floors.

ALEXANDER TURNBULL LIBRARY

BELOW

The Wellington Provincial Council Building was designed by Christian Toxward in 1871. Plans had already been in existence for such a building since 1865. Toxward's building provided space for a large debating chamber, a Bellamy's restaurant, numerous committee rooms and offices for the provincial departments. As this was a building of some public importance, a grand foundation stone laying ceremony was held with tiered seating for the spectators, beflagged ships in the harbour and a 'brilliant display of bunting on extemporised flag poles' (*Evening Post*, January 1872). The building was constructed in native timber and all the furnishings were made in Wellington — a boost for local industry and a source of great pride for Wellington's inhabitants.

In 1893, the building was sold for removal for £145 to make room for a new Government Life Insurance office, which was replaced in 1934 by the present Government Life building.

ALEXANDER TURNBULL LIBRARY

93

In 1877 Thomas Turnbull designed these splendid brick and plaster offices for the Wellington City Council on the corner of Featherston and Brandon Streets, now the site of the Alliance Assurance building. It was built with a marked absence of problems and was opened with a similarly marked absence of public acclaim, save for a big dinner held in its central hall.

After the City Council moved its offices to the new Town Hall, it leased this building for commercial use. It became widely known as Gaulter's Building (after the lessee) until it, and its neighbouring buildings, were demolished in the late 1950s.

ALEXANDER TURNBULL LIBRARY

OPPOSITE

Although the Government Life Insurance had opened its doors to policy holders in 1869, it did not start building its own premises until 1893, on the site of the Wellington Provincial Council Chambers in which it had been a tenant. Eight years earlier, in 1885, a design competition had been announced for a new building and had been won by a young architect, Joshua Charlesworth, who worked on his plans in a hut while supervising road works in the Auckland district. Charlesworth later moved to Wellington to practise, but his design for the Government Life building was never used. Instead, Frederick Clere (in partnership as Clere, FitzGerald and Richmond) designed the building. He produced an edifice of singular appearance with its red brick walls, limestone trim, complex roofline and slightly Gothic styling.

Construction was carried out in two stages, commencing with the two side wings then progressing to the central block. The *Evening Post* described the building as 'perhaps the most striking edifice in the city' (November 1892) and Clere's drawings of it were exhibited at the Academy of Arts for public perusal. The building was lit by electricity and had wide corridors for maximum natural light. It was roofed with imported slate, and heated by hot water pipes which obviated the need for open fires. It was demolished in 1932 and replaced by the present Government Life building designed by John Mair.

ALEXANDER TURNBULL LIBRARY

This photograph of the Public Trust building on Lambton Quay shows the final design drawn up by John Campbell in April 1906. As early as 1901 test bores had been done on the site to determine the foundation type required, and drawings were underway. Campbell had returned from a study trip to the United States and Europe and brought back with him an enthusiasm for steel-framed buildings. The Public Trust Office was to be his first venture into this new construction method.

Delays then set in, during which time the government toyed with the idea of allowing an American firm to design and build the office. They decided against this option because of expense. By 1906 Campbell had drawn up new plans incorporating a mansard roof and using Tonga Bay granite for the base, and construction began. The contract price was £41,000 and the builders, J. and A. Wilson, had a factory built in Stout Street to do all the steel and stone work. The building was opened in mid-1909, and the *Evening Post* declared, 'there is no stucco, no cheap make-believe about the impressive office.' It went on to muse, 'the only tawdry feature about the whole structure lies at the top of the dome in the little gilt sphere that supports the flagstaff.'
ALEXANDER TURNBULL LIBRARY

OPPOSITE

This photograph, taken about 1870, shows the austere wooden post office built in 1862. The *Wellington Independent* described its style as the plainest Italian, indeed, 'rather too plain for our fancy' (January 1862). Its time ball, commissioned in 1864, was dropped every day except Sunday at midday.

This building and its close neighbour the Customs House (out of the view) was added to over the years and finally sold for removal for £140 in 1882 to allow site works for the new post office.
AUTHOR

97

Wellington's General Post Office was designed by Thomas Turnbull in 1882 and completed in record time. Its piles were made of totara wood from the forests near Carterton and driven four metres to bedrock. The base was made of concrete, the walls were brick, and the clocktower was wooden. By mid-1883 the building was ready except for the clock. A heated battle arose over who should pay for it. While the argument continued one enterprising merchant applied to pay a rental to advertise pork sausages and merino mutton on the clockless tower. Finally, it was decided the cost of the clock should be shared between the government and the city. The Minister of Public Works then decided to alter Turnbull's design of the tower, with the result that the bells sounded muffled. The *Evening Post* suggested this was 'probably the greatest and proudest achievement of his ministerial career' (April 1884).

Early one morning in April 1887 the building was totally gutted by a fire which might have been arrested had government retrenchment not resulted in the building's nightwatchman being laid off just a week previously. The government decided to restore the building at a cost of £14,000, but was slow to begin. In the interim thieves were able to make off with the melted bronze from the bells. The ruined shell was considered both dangerous and ugly. 'If the ruins are to be left unrepaired,' mused the *Evening Post* (November 1887), 'then no time should be lost in planting the ivy which would make them picturesque.'

The government resolved not to replace the clock-tower, a decision that incensed Wellingtonians, and firm protests were made. The government then revoked its decision with the proviso that the cost of the tower and the bells be borne solely by the city.

In 1974 this building was demolished and the site was to lie vacant for fourteen years before being redeveloped.
AUTHOR

One of the first lavish hotels offering everything from private suites to large dining rooms was the Theatre Royal Hotel on the corner of Lambton Quay and Johnston Street. It was designed in 1876 by Thomas Turnbull as a single building. Its Lambton Quay frontage consisted of two adjacent buildings of two and three floors. It was built in the face of hostility from nearby hotel owners who disliked the idea of competition. It cost £4,000 to build and boasted public apartments including a luxurious oyster saloon, a parlour bar, a commercial room, a billiard room and a huge dining room upstairs. It also had fifteen bedrooms. Soon after its completion it was renamed the Oxford Hotel. Its interior was completely refitted in 1886 to make both sections three-storeyed. It then became better known as the Club Hotel.

To the right of the hotel on Johnston Street is the Theatre Royal, designed in 1872 by Christian Toxward. It became linked to the hotel, providing easy access for intermission refreshments. The theatre was supplied with four different grades of seating: the pit, boxes, dress circle and a vice-regal box. It could accommodate 600 people seated and had standing room for 400. The pit area was set on hydraulic lifts so that its floor could be raised to the level of the stage for public meetings.

The large domed ceiling was fitted with a gas-lit sunburst in its centre, which was intricately painted with etiolating rays and fitted with hundreds of small mirrors for a spangled effect.

The hotel and theatre were demolished in 1915 to make way for the Midland Hotel, which was in turn replaced by the Midland Park in 1982.
AUTHOR

OPPOSITE

The top photograph shows the Occidental Hotel on the corner of Lambton Quay and Johnston Street. It was designed in 1873 by Christian Toxward and three years later it was doubled to the size shown here. Just discernible to the left is the only private house constructed on the reclaimed land. It was built for Dr Diver in 1874 to designs by Toxward and was demolished in 1906. In 1908 the hotel was sold for removal to make way for part of the present Kirkcaldie and Stains block.
TYREE COLLECTION, ALEXANDER TURNBULL LIBRARY

At right is the Oriental Hotel in Willis Street, designed in 1876 by Charles Tringham and originally called the Melbourne Hotel. It was one of Willis Street's tallest buildings and required substantial excavation of the hill behind it. This interference with the escarpment resulted in a massive slip of 300 tons of rock, which all but demolished the hotel's dining room.

In 1901 the hotel was destroyed by fire, resulting in one death, and a fearful scramble to safety. The place was overcrowded and people were even sleeping in shake-downs. An inquiry was held and was very damning of the fire alarms and escapes. It was reported that the hotel had long since been served notice of improvements which were never made. A replacement hotel was built, designed by George Schwartz, and was known variously as the Palace and the Carlton until its recent demolition.

ALEXANDER TURNBULL LIBRARY

OPPOSITE

In 1876 the Union Bank sold their premises at the corner of Willis and Boulcott Streets to John Plimmer for £4,300. Soon after, Plimmer designed a hotel called the Albert for the site and incorporated much of the bank building into the hotel. Although the hotel's official name was the Albert, it was more commonly known as the Old Identities, and for good reason. Plimmer indulged his penchant for whimsy, and had masks of local celebrities placed as keystones to the upper floor windows. On top of the pediment over the main entrance in Willis Street, to the left, was a statue of Edward Wakefield.

This hotel was not Plimmer's sole excursion into architectural whimsy. He had turned the damaged ship the *Inconstant* into the 'Noah's Ark' warehouse on Lambton Quay. He was also the proud owner of a large carved dove above the entrance to his own house on Plimmer Steps — yet another symbol of the great flood.

In 1929 the Albert Hotel was demolished and the St George Hotel was built on the site.

TYREE COLLECTION, ALEXANDER TURNBULL LIBRARY

The Grand Hotel in Willis Street was among the last of the large hotels to be built in colonial Wellington. It was designed in 1904 by James O'Dea on the site of the Commercial Hotel (later known as the Western), which had opened its doors in 1875. Soon after construction began it was decided to add an extra two floors onto the original four-storeyed design, making it one of the tallest buildings in the city on its opening in late 1906. The opening was celebrated by a huge house-warming reception, for which a thousand invitations were sent out. Utterly up to date, the Grand offered 110 bedrooms, all with gas heating and many supplied with telephones. The main dining room had seating for 100 guests. A special feature of the building was its flat roof, which was used as a promenade and was reached by swift electric lifts. Such hotels were well patronised and offered significant employment. The Grand, for example, had a staff of nearly forty-five.

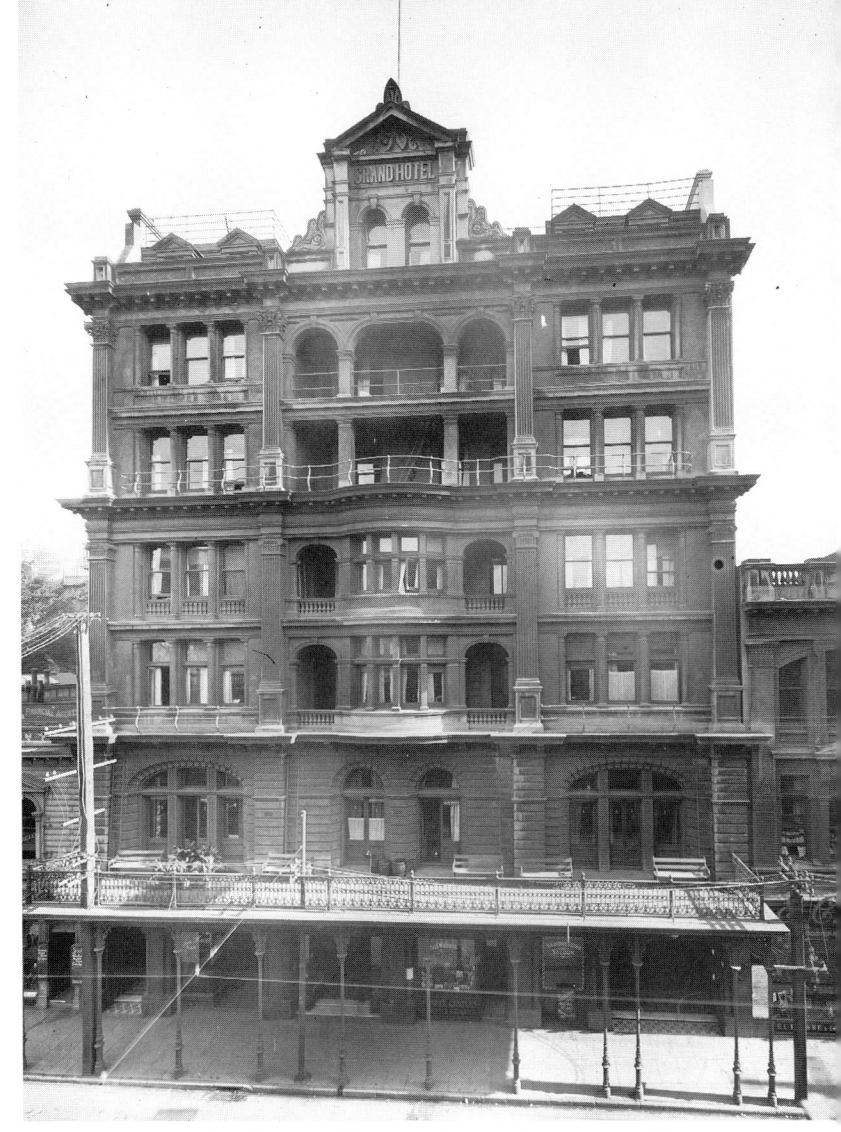

The site is now occupied by the Grand Arcade and office tower.

S. C. SMITH COLLECTION, ALEXANDER TURNBULL LIBRARY

St Paul's in Mulgrave Street was built in 1866 to designs by Frederick Thatcher, who was also at one time its minister. The Anglican Bishop at the time, Charles Abraham, said that 'being built of totara, it [the cathedral] may last, unless some accident occurs to it, several centuries.' It replaced an earlier church built in 1844 on what is now part of Parliament grounds, and its original shape was little more than an oblong. Within eighteen months it was found necessary to strengthen the building because it was greatly exposed to the wind. A south transept designed by Christian Toxward was built in 1868, and in 1873 a north transept and aisle, also by Toxward, were added. These additions, and numerous others in subsequent decades, helped to stabilise the building and increase its seating capacity. They also produced an interior which has drawn favourable comment from architectural observers, particularly for its ceiling work.

Its function as a cathedral church has been superseded by the present cathedral on Molesworth Street. It is now known and cherished as Old St Paul's.

E. R. WILLIAMS COLLECTION, ALEXANDER TURNBULL LIBRARY

In the centre of this photograph of Lambton Quay, taken about 1870, is the Second Presbyterian Church, St Andrew's, known at the time as the Scotch Church. It was built in 1866 as a replacement for an earlier church that was sold and moved across the road to become a shop. To help pay for building the new church a two-day bazaar was held in the Athenaeum, (to the left of the church), raising a substantial £250.

Although the sides are quite plain, the front facade boasts a pleasant Classical style with a large coloured window (made in Dunedin) and a steeple in which provision had been made to install a public clock. In 1878 the church trustees sold their land to the Colonial Bank for a staggering £10,000. The church was sold for removal and later used as an Anglican Sunday School on Tinakori Road.

A replacement St Andrew's was built on the Terrace to designs by Christian Toxward, but it was destroyed by fire in 1918.

ALEXANDER TURNBULL LIBRARY

Hill Street was the locus of much Catholic activity and over the years a number of church buildings were erected in this area — the Catholic Bishops' Court, St Mary's School and Convent, St Joseph's Orphanage, and the Pro-cathedral of St Mary's. Originally little more than a barn, St Mary's soon became a prominent landmark after it was enlarged to designs by Christian Toxward in 1866 at a cost of £3,000. Toxward also added extra aisles, strengthened the structure with flying buttresses, and gave it a splendid bell tower. The additions made the exterior look grand but the interior was not refitted and decorated until 1878. A ceiling of grained oak was installed, stained glass arrived from France for the sanctuary, and a high altar of coloured marble was commissioned in Paris. This interior work was carried out by a local engineer, Charles O'Neill.

In November 1898 St Mary's was destroyed by fire. The crowds assembling to watch reported that the gilded statue of Our Lady, set thirty metres above the ground in a niche in the tower, floated slowly and safely to the ground. After the fire, subscription lists were opened for rebuilding, headed by an offer of £1,050 from Mr and Mrs Martin Kennedy and supported by many parishes throughout the country. The architect was Francis Petre of Dunedin. Building of the new church began in 1899 at a cost of £9,000. Fire and earthquake-proof materials of iron-strengthened concrete were used and the pressed bricks and Marseilles tile roof made it a notable structure.

ALEXANDER TURNBULL LIBRARY

In 1847 the first St Peter's Anglican Church, designed by Henry Cridland, was built on the corner of Willis and Ghuznee Streets. By the 1870s it had been added to four times and ended up looking like a 'large, straggling, disproportionate, shapeless, hideous deformity' (*Evening Post*, April 1879).

In 1877 a new church was designed by architect M. A. E. Grosholz, who died the following year, aged twenty-seven. Thomas Turnbull was then appointed supervising architect. He found Grosholz's plans unsatisfactory, with numerous omissions and a dangerously weak tower. He was asked to design a new church, shown in the photograph. The old church was moved back on the site in 1879, a foundation stone laying ceremony performed after twice being postponed by bad weather, and construction went smoothly. The only defect in the design of the church was that the tower was found to be too weak to cope with the stresses of swinging bells, so they had to be struck instead.

St Peter's still stands as a central city church.

ALEXANDER TURNBULL LIBRARY

In 1869 the Jewish community had their synagogue built on the Terrace to designs by Christian Toxward. It was built in wood along the stylistic lines of a small Greek temple. The engraving of the Hebrew words Beth-El (House of God) above the front door prevented it from looking like a small branch of a bank. Its interior, seating 170, was all white plaster picked out with gilded ornament, while the alcove for the Scrolls was enclosed by white satin curtains with fringes of silver bullion. Down a narrow alley to one side of the building was the Rabbi's house, overlooking a bush-clad valley. Here in Glencoe Avenue lived Wellington's most celebrated Rabbi, Herman Van Staveren, who led the Jewish community for fifty-three years from the time of his arrival in 1877.

Toxward's synagogue was the first non-residential building on the Terrace, although it was joined by churches for the Presbyterians and Congregationalists within a few decades.

In 1928 the building was demolished and a new brick synagogue was built on the site. This has also disappeared, as the approach of the motorway in the late 1960s led to a new Jewish Centre being built in Webb Street.

NATIONAL MUSEUM, WELLINGTON, NEG. B 13203

This photograph shows Wellington's first Congregational Church before demolition in 1908. Situated at the top of Woodward Street, it was just a stone's throw to Lambton Quay (then washed by harbour tides), yet it also nestled under the long escarpment of Wellington Terrace. The building served the Congregationalists until 1887 when they moved to their new church building on the corner of the Terrace and Bowen Street. It was a much bigger structure, the cost of which was largely met by selling the Woodward Street property on a rising commercial land market. The 1849 building was subsequently used as a brewery, and a bulk warehouse.

AUCKLAND WEEKLY NEWS

This photograph shows the stern face and nondescript sides of the Supreme Court on Lambton Quay, designed in 1862 by Charles Carter. Nestling under an escarpment of rock, it was referred to as a 'heavy headed monster frowning with overhanging brows' by one correspondent to the *Wellington Independent*. Built for £4,300, it provided accommodation for the Supreme and Magistrates Courts, holding cells, various offices and the police station. In 1878, the building and land went up for auction and were bought for £16,400 by Walter Buller, who leased them to the government.

Four years later he sold them to the Bank of New South Wales and after being refitted, the building was opened as their banking premises. In 1904 it was sold for removal for £180 to make way for a new bank building. Some magnificent pohutukawa trees which grew in front were transplanted to the Botanic Garden.

ALEXANDER TURNBULL LIBRARY

This photograph by W. H. Davis shows the ornate structure of the newly completed Supreme Court on Stout Street. The building is surrounded by an iron fence, which seemed to be standard issue for government buildings at that time. Within weeks of its opening the interior of the main court was criticised for its confusing layout and poor acoustics, and deemed 'simply wretched' by the *Evening Post* (April 1881). The acoustics problem was rectified to some extent by draping the windows and dais with about 370 metres of heavy cloth imported from England — although this took nearly three years to arrive.

A new police station was built on the Lambton Quay frontage of the court precinct in 1880. It had plenty of offices and sleeping quarters, but evidently it did not 'enter into the mind of the Colonial Architect to include a kitchen' (*New Zealand Mail*, January 1881). The problem was solved by snugly fitting a galvanised iron cookhouse between the station and the courthouse.

Mounds of shingle used to surface the city streets can be seen in the foreground. Arduous relief work was provided for the city's unemployed, who were engaged on a daily basis to break the shingle down into manageable grades.

ELLIS COLLECTION, ALEXANDER TURNBULL LIBRARY

The buildings of Wellington's Terrace Jail were extensive. This photograph, taken about 1905, shows the prominent three-storeyed brick block of sixty cells designed in 1902 by William Hales, the colony's Engineer-in-Chief. Also visible are the neatly planted vegetable gardens. Many of the other buildings in the photograph date from 1875, when Christian Toxward designed several additions to the jail, which at that time had already been standing for twenty years. The whole complex was hidden from view by belts of conifers grown in the Botanic Garden's pinetum.

This jail held many prisoners sentenced to terms of hard labour. The sight of gangs of prisoners going out to work each day around the city was not easily forgotten by the residents. The annual worth of each prisoner's labour was about £75, while the annual cost of keeping each prisoner was about £45. It was little wonder hard labour kept operating and was acceptable to the public.

ALEXANDER TURNBULL LIBRARY

This photograph of the Mt Cook Jail was taken in 1907, by which time it was being used as a military barracks. Of fearful proportions and constructed with relentless solidity, it was intended as a prison for Wellington and the greater Central Districts. Described as a 'vast human cage' by the *New Zealand Times* (January 1897), its interior consisted of three storeys of single cells. The walls were reinforced with massive straps of iron. The *New Zealand Times* reporter who visited it in 1897 found it a chilling place and reported that the women's section was like a dungeon in which 'no gentlemen would dream of stabling his horse.'

It was dismantled in the early 1930s. The site is now occupied by the National Art Gallery and Museum.

AUCKLAND WEEKLY NEWS

ABOVE

This hospital in Thorndon was a replacement for a brick building badly damaged in the 1848 earthquake. For close to three decades it was a centre for major surgery and an institution for the sick poor. By the 1870s there were strong calls for a new building as this structure had become dilapidated with its 'timber turned to honey-comb and dust' (*Evening Post*, November 1872). Its roof was leaking, the floor had decayed, ventilation was poor, and the drainage appalling, with a patients' cess-pool barely a few metres away from the building.

While the new hospital was being built at Newtown, the Thorndon building deteriorated even further. After its patients were moved in 1881, the Thorndon land was cut up for lease as house sites.

ELLIS COLLECTION, ALEXANDER TURNBULL LIBRARY

BELOW

In June 1881 the new hospital was opened with a grand ball. The building was decorated with Chinese lanterns and seating areas were dotted about the gardens. About 500 guests attended the function. The supper was donated by local merchants on the urging of a ladies' committee. After the ball leftovers were distributed, the 'lighter delicacies to patients and the more substantial viands to the poor' (*Evening Post*, June 1881). Built at a cost of £45,000 (exclusive of seven years' prison labour) and furnished from England, the building had four large wards (each with twenty-four beds), and along the sunny front face were six furnished rooms for private patients. In front of the main entrance was a large fountain with ornamental basins and rockwork bases. When the wind was not overly strong, the fountain ejected streams of water higher than the building itself.

ALEXANDER TURNBULL LIBRARY

In 1885 a local branch of the Order of St John of Jerusalem was established in Wellington to provide ambulance transport for accident victims. Until then, victims were often bundled into cabs and taken to hospital or the nearest doctor, which must have complicated many injuries. The St John's Ambulance Association was well supported and had, at first, a litter available for use, which was housed in the Brandon Street Fire Station. In 1900 they took delivery of a horse-drawn ambulance imported from England. The Association established a Nursing Guild in 1902, assisted by the donation and enthusiasm of local benefactress Sarah Rhodes. It was then able to provide home nursing care and material help to the distressed and poor. However, a public contribution was also needed, and once a year collectors would go out onto the streets on 'Ambulance Saturday'. At that time Saturday was one of the busiest shopping days. This photograph shows two collectors on Lambton Quay in 1908 helping raise £300 for that year. Such support was a reflection of the Association's standing. They treated about 5,000 patients every year, and were thus a familiar name to the public.

WEEKLY PRESS

The chemists of the day offered the public a huge range of medicines and preparations of varying efficacy. This photograph shows the Te Aro Dispensary on the corner of Manners and Herbert Streets. The dispensary started life as a small octagonal building called the Pill Box, built in the 1840s as a branch establishment for Charles Barraud. Part of this Pill Box is visible to the right down Herbert Street. It was eventually bought by Henry Brittain, who carried out additions in the late 1870s, creating a curious appearance with decorative window surrounds, urns along the parapet, a splendid verandah and any amount of sign-writing. Brittain ran a large prescribing business and stocked a vast list of proprietary medicines, including popular lines like Brittain's Headache Powder, Nervine for toothache, Irish Moss, Vermifuge, Corn and Wart Cure and White Worm Powder.

The building no longer exists, and nor does its replacement of 1909. The site is now part of present-day Victoria Street.

ALEXANDER TURNBULL LIBRARY

Several hundred people attended the opening of Mother Aubert's Home of Compassion at Island Bay in April 1907. The Home of Compassion had begun in Buckle Street and relied totally on public kindness to assist a sector of the population not provided for by the hospitals or charitable agencies. Of much concern to Mother Aubert and her helpers were children abandoned for such reasons as illegitimacy and parent desertion. This work was sometimes questioned by the self-righteous, but was nevertheless widely supported by the public. The sight of Mother Aubert and her helpers collecting food and clothes in large prams around the city was a familiar one until the First World War.

The building at Island Bay, designed by James O'Dea and costing £33,000, provided accommodation for 150 children on its opening. Numerous ancillary buildings have assured it a continued existence.

On opening day so many people wanted to get onto the flat roof (designed as a promenade) that their weight caused a severe structural weakness. Repairing the damage was an unexpected drain on already limited funds. The public donated money both for furnishing the building and constructing the water reservoir on the hills behind — a task achieved by volunteers (including the colony's Governor) carting 200 tons of material up the hill by hand.

S. C. SMITH COLLECTION, ALEXANDER TURNBULL LIBRARY

This view of the Porirua Asylum shows a section of the vast main building designed by the Government Architect, John Campbell, in 1891 and built in several stages. The asylum site had been purchased seven years earlier and the patients moved there were engaged in landscaping and planting gardens. Built from prison-made bricks and roofed with Welsh slate, this building was completed in 1895. By 1900 two new brick wings had been completed and the institution expanded its capacity to 500 patients. A network of other buildings was erected on the site over the years, giving it the appearance of a large agricultural estate. The brick buildings were demolished in 1944.
AUCKLAND WEEKLY NEWS

OPPOSITE
In 1868 Christian Toxward designed a building for the Wellington Grammar and Commercial School — later Wellington College — on a site on Clifton Terrace leased from the City Council on its Town Belt. The school had been granted land in 1853 for rental purposes but its first building did not open its doors to pupils until 1867, in the Woodward Street Congregational Schoolroom. A year later it moved to a military building on land that later became Fitzherbert Terrace. In 1868 a contract for about £1,000 was let for the building illustrated, as well as the necessary site excavations and roading up to it. Toxward's Gothic-styled building had three large rooms, each heated by open fireplaces, and open roofs reaching over seven metres at their ridges. It could accommodate 200 pupils, but when it opened in late 1868 it had only fifty pupils whose parents had paid the annual fee of £12. In 1878 the building was enlarged with two wings; by this time it was no longer the Wellington College, but the Terrace School for Infants. It was burnt down in 1901 after being used as a barracks during the visit of the Duke and Duchess of Cornwall and York to Wellington. Rebuilt as a school by William Turnbull in 1902, it was subsequently demolished when the motorway altered the topography of this area of the Terrace.
EVENING POST COLLECTION, ALEXANDER TURNBULL LIBRARY

This building, the fourth home of Wellington College, was designed by Christian Toxward in 1872 on part of a Town Belt reserve abutting the suburb of Mt Victoria on one side and the Mt View Asylum on the other. Large-scale site excavations were carried out by hard labour gangs, who were treated to a Christmas dinner by the school's governors when the work was finished. The building cost nearly £1,000, which included items such as fencing, drainage, furniture and servants' quarters, but excluded the two wings, one of which appears in this photograph taken in 1874. The elaborate Gothic style was thought to be 'apparently a blending of the middle-pointed and Tudor varieties' by the *Evening Post* in July 1873. A tall spire was planned for the tower, but in the end it was just finished with a steep mansard dome. 'There is a large room in the tower to which access had not yet been provided, although this had been contemplated,' reported the *New Zealand Times* in June 1874.

Apart from classrooms and the rather majestic residence for the headmaster, the wing to the right, the school building also had a large lecture hall on the first floor, finished in native timbers and sporting a high Gothic-detailed ceiling. After the second wing had been completed in 1883, Toxward's building remained substantially the same until its demolition in 1930.

ALEXANDER TURNBULL LIBRARY

The 1870s saw some interesting developments in the country's education. In 1877 free, compulsory primary schooling was introduced. This required some heavy expenditure on school buildings, and the various Education Boards appointed architects to prepare school designs for them. The first architect appointed to the Wellington Education Board was Christian Toxward. In 1875 he designed the Mt Cook Infants' School in the photograph. It was situated on Buckle Street, near the Armed Constabulary depot. The Gothic style was considered appropriate at that time. This was one of three schools built for the densely populated Mt Cook area. By the early 1930s all three schools had amalgamated and shifted to a single new school high up on the south end of the Terrace near the city's jail.

NATIONAL MUSEUM, WELLINGTON, NEG. B 9769

In 1885 part of the old hospital grounds in Thorndon was proclaimed the site of a girls' high school. Thomas Turnbull drew up plans for an imposing building to accommodate 200 pupils and to be built either in wood or brick, depending on the tender prices received. The price of £4,500 from contractors Scoullar and Archibald was accepted and the building went up in wood, somewhat to the dismay of local commentators who though the site was too good, and the institution too useful, for a mere wooden building. Opened late in 1887, it was typical of many school buildings of the time. The room heights were generous — almost five metres — and were difficult to heat. Like many schools, funding was tight and often subject to government retrenchment. 'Luxuries' such as libraries and any specialised equipment (for everything from gymnasia to museums) were funded by donation and money-raising.

In the case of the Wellington Girls' High School, fundraising was also required to get the playing grounds into some order. When the school opened, they were strewn with rags, bones, tins and broken crockery. The *New Zealand Mail* (February 1888) found the surroundings 'like the dreary exercise yard of a prison.'

Turnbull's building was demolished in 1970 to allow construction of a new tower block for the school.
ALEXANDER TURNBULL LIBRARY

Education was of great concern to the Catholic Church and their involvement with schools was strong in towns with a significant Catholic presence. In 1876 Thomas Turnbull was asked to design two schools for the Wellington diocese: St Mary's in Hill Street, and the Marist Brothers School in Boulcott Street, photographed here. A delightful Italian-styled building, it possessed one large central room with others leading off it, connected by folding doors. Because of the sloping of the site, Turnbull was also able to incorporate living quarters for the Brothers into the design without upsetting its visual balance. The fine tower was not solely ornamental. In 1878 the Catholic Bishop signed a Deed of Grant allowing the City Council to use the tower as a fire look-out.

The building was demolished in 1934 and the site remained empty for almost fifty years.

NATIONAL MUSEUM, WELLINGTON, NEG. B 12195

OPPOSITE

This photograph shows the first block built for Victoria University. For some time it had held its lectures in a variety of leased premises. It had also been the focus of sharp and lengthy debate over a suitable site for its permanent home. The site in Kelburn Parade was finally chosen in 1902 and the following year a design competition for a building was held. To ensure impartiality, the nine entries were sent to a Melbourne architect, whose name was not divulged, for judging. The winners were Francis Penty and Edward Blake, who shared the £100 prize and remained together as the firm Penty and Blake. They were required to show two versions — one of a finished building costing £30,000, and one of what could be built immediately for £15,000. The contract was won by Allan McGuire for £25,000, and by 1904 work had begun on the central portion and science block shown in the photograph. This block now forms part of the much cherished and extended Hunter Building.

NATIONAL MUSEUM, WELLINGTON

This early photograph clearly shows the great scale of the Oddfellows Hall on Lambton Quay in relation to the townsfolk. Built in 1859, it became one of the city's favourite gathering places, especially for visiting entertainers. In 1865 it was used for performances by the Lyster Opera Company; in 1869 Dr Carr gave a show of mesmeric seances and 'electro-psychological phenomena'; 1870 saw both Woodruffe's 'fancy and philosophical' glassblowing, and Kreitmayer's waxwork figures; and in 1875 the Fakir of Oolu performed tricks there, assisted by a 'beautiful entranced lady'.

In 1878 Thomas Turnbull completely remodelled the front of the building in brick, providing shops and offices, and the large hall inside became known as the Academy of Music. In 1881 further alterations were made. The front became the premises of the Colonial Insurance Company and the interior was refitted for the Central Club.

The site is now occupied by the T and G Building.

WELLINGTON PUBLIC LIBRARY

The Athenaeum, designed by Turnbull, can be seen at the left of this photograph of Lambton Quay, taken in 1878. The foundation stone was laid in 1877 in a ceremony for ticket-holders only. 'It is to be regretted,' said the *New Zealand Mail* (June 1877), 'that the order for the trowel had to be sent to Dunedin instead of being executed by Wellington artizans.' The institution was dogged by money problems. Despite suggestions of imposing public subscriptions, introducing charges for non-members, and persuading the City Council to waive payment of rates, the Athenaeum got further into financial difficulties and was roundly criticised for the way it was run. 'Every latitude has been given to the Athenaeum authorities by the great ones of Wellington,' declared the *New Zealand Mail* (January 1881), yet the reading room was found to be 'slovenly arranged and the files ridiculously incomplete.' The Athenaeum was demolished in 1933 to make way for the present Prudential building.

To the right of the Athenaeum is one of Turnbull's pioneering exercises in plastered brick design. The building, designed in 1878, was for the Colonial Bank. Reinforced with cast iron girders through the brick walls, the building contained two premises, one of which was leased by the Colonial Bank to the South British Insurance Company. These premises were also demolished in the 1930s to make way for the Commercial Bank of Australia and the Guardian Trust.

ALEXANDER TURNBULL LIBRARY

The Wellington Public Library was designed in 1890 by William Crichton, who later became a partner with James McKay in the prolific firm Crichton and McKay. This photo shows the first wing to be erected. The building was constructed with hollow walls to ensure dryness and had a 'floating' foundation, as the land was reclaimed from the harbour. It was opened in 1893 and was open from 10 a.m. to 10 p.m. every day of the week. The Athenaeum books and magazines were deposited here, donations were sought and local booksellers Lyon and Blair secured the contract for supplying books from overseas.

In 1894 an earthquake hit Wellington and damaged the building. The restitution architects, Thomas Turnbull and William Chatfield, had the tower removed, criticised the 'floating' foundations, declaring they should have been solid and down to bedrock, and introduced iron tension rods throughout the roofs.

In 1904 another earthquake damaged the building, throwing down half a ton of decorative pediment, reducing the reference room on the top floor to a mass of plaster and books, and pushing the back wall out of plumb. The Mayor promptly closed the building, and cordoned off the area. The City Engineer was entrusted with the expensive task of restoring it a second time.

The library site now forms part of the revamped Civic Centre area. The building to the left at the rear of the library was Thomas Turnbull's Education Board Offices, designed in 1890 and now the site of the present City Council building.

ALEXANDER TURNBULL LIBRARY

This photograph, taken in 1880, shows the Colonial Museum on Museum Street, designed by William Clayton in 1874. To the right, tucked away in its own garden, is the house of the director, James Hector, built in 1865. The iron fence surrounding the precinct was put up in 1876 and was virtually standard issue for government buildings, much to the scathing criticism of the press. The institution was a popular one, with about seventy visitors a day during the late 1870s. Later it became shabby and overcrowded, and by the first years of the new century there were strong demands for a new building. Reporters went to visit the museum from time to time. In January 1905 they thought the place 'poky and out-of-date', and when inspecting the galleries upstairs found it was like rummaging in the 'attic of some taxidermist's shop.' In another visit in May 1906 reporters described the building as the 'miserable abode of the lords and ladies of the animal world, the jewels of the earth's crust, the gems of fine art. Their claim is a palace, and they are given a garret.'

In 1907, the press reported that the government had decided to rebuild the museum on the Mt Cook reserve, but added, 'it will be some time before the structure appears on the commanding site' (*Evening Post*, September 1907). Indeed, it took twenty-five years.

ALEXANDER TURNBULL LIBRARY

This view of the main entrance to the Botanic Garden on Tinakori Road shows some of the existing growth on the site and the rough nature of Tinakori Road, which even then was the main route to Karori. One of the Garden's functions was to test crops for commercial use in the colony. Over a number of years plants such as flax, silkworm mulberries, cork oak, sugar cane, olive trees and hops were experimented with. The Botanic Garden was also used as a trial ground for forestry, and a variety of conifers including species from California, Australia and the Himalayas were grown in the pinetum. The Garden served as a nursery, raising and distributing hundreds of thousands of trees and plants to local councils, government departments, and private individuals. One popular feature was the 'teaching garden' of the 1880s, with its numerous oblong beds of flowers all edged with box hedges and surrounded by trellis fencing to dissuade vandalism. It is now the site of the sound shell.

ALEXANDER TURNBULL LIBRARY

A favourite private garden of colonial Wellington was 'Bellevue' in the Hutt Valley. The house and garden were originally established in 1847 by botanist-settler Alfred Ludlam, and called 'Newry'. Ludlam was a prolific importer of rare plants from nurseries all over the world. On his death in 1877, the four hectares of gardens, three hectares of orchard, seven hectares of lawns, and the house, were bought by James McNab. McNab once owned a nursery in Thorndon, and on buying 'Newry', opened it to the public for a charge. Known as McNab's Gardens, it was sold in 1896 to the Ross family, who continued to open it to the public. In 1900 it went up for auction both as pleasure gardens and as a subdivision of fifty-five villa sections called Ludlum Park. The pleasure gardens were bought for £5,000 by Orr and Lodder, hoteliers who had owned the high class City Buffet on Lambton Quay — later the Gresham Hotel. Orr and Lodder renamed the place 'Bellevue', and extended the house to include a twenty-five-bedroom wing and a dining room seating 300. The additions were designed by William Chatfield and completed in 1905.

Later the grounds were subdivided further, the hotel fell into disrepair and was finally destroyed by fire.

ALEXANDER TURNBULL LIBRARY

OPPOSITE

On the original town map of Wellington the Basin Reserve was earmarked for use as an inland harbour with access to the sea by way of the strip of land between Kent and Cambridge Terraces. However, the 1855 earthquake lifted up the land, and the reserve, while swampy, was designated for public use. It was drained and levelled by prison labour and by the mid-1860s had been fenced and planted around with a thorn hedge. It was leased out to the Cricket Association who, along with the Caledonian Society, kept it in repair and had the first grandstand built. This view, taken about 1885, shows a fairly level playing ground and part of the bandstand from which popular music was regularly played.

Overlooking the reserve are the Wellington College (on the right), St Mark's Anglican Church designed by Charles Tringham in 1876 (in the middle), and the grand house of engineer John Rees George, built in 1877 (on the left).

ALEXANDER TURNBULL LIBRARY

Sport and recreation were just as enthusiastically organised as any other social institution in Wellington, and they faced similar difficulties of funding. Swimming, cricket and racing were perhaps the most widely supported. However, the city's four bowling clubs (Thorndon, Mt Victoria, Newtown and Te Aro) were also strongly supported. This photograph shows the Wellington Bowling Club's pavilion at the Te Aro green in Aro Street (then called Wordsworth Street). It was built for £1,700 in 1907 to designs by Edward Blake and with its members' amenities, spectators' seating and players' greens it was considered 'one of the handsomest and most commodious [bowling clubs] in Australasia' by the *Auckland Weekly News* (October 1907). It was demolished in the late 1960s, and the site is now occupied by a complex of rental housing.
AUCKLAND WEEKLY NEWS

ABOVE

This particularly engaging building was the Thorndon public baths, built in 1898 to designs by Joshua Charlesworth. The architectural style is reminiscent of much public recreation architecture of the turn of the century.

The baths proved a popular amenity for both private swimmers and organised events, with facilities like changing sheds, supervision, tiered seating and refreshment rooms. It also helped to put an end to the roundly scorned practice of nude bathing.

Harbour reclamations have removed this building and the Thorndon Esplanade from the city map.
WELLINGTON PUBLIC LIBRARY

BELOW

Across the harbour from Wellington lay numerous small bays whose benefit for both residential and recreational use were widely acknowledged towards the turn of the century. The building illustrated is the Days Bay Pavilion, designed by William Chatfield in 1897 and built for £2,000. It was built for local merchant J. H. Williams, whose landholding in the area ran to about 280 hectares, and who instituted a steam ferry service across the harbour with two well-known vessels, the *Duco* and *Duchess*. The pavilion was opened in January 1898 with a dance, and it became a favourite place for excursions by groups of friends or employees treated by their employers. Its popularity was evident by the number of people using it, particularly during the summer. In the season of its opening, over 10,000 people were taken by steamer. Williams, the son of a pioneer who made a fortune supplying coal to Wellington, soon added to the building. He also provided an amusement park which had a water slide at the rear of the pavilion. Bought by the Wellington Ferry Company in 1900, then administered by the City Council, the pavilion was destroyed by fire in October 1952.
WELLINGTON PUBLIC LIBRARY

Wellington's Town Hall was designed by Joshua Charlesworth in 1900. It was built in plastered brick at a time when there was such a shortage of bricks in the city that on at least one occasion the contractor had to lay off the workers. Plasterers were also in short supply as their services were in great demand. A number had been brought over from Australia to work on the building.

Soon after construction started several changes were made to the design; the ornamentation was embellished, and the portico was raised to prevent traffic from pulling up directly at the front doors. Problems persisted after it opened in late 1904. The plasterwork tended to go black from the soot pouring out of the New Zealand Electrical Syndicate's powerhouse opposite. Damp floors had to be dried out by lighting fires in the basement and boring holes through the brickwork to improve ventilation. The clock intended for the tower did not arrive until 1923. It was a gift to the city from John Blundell, and is now installed in the Central Fire Station.

The Town Hall is still standing today but in 1934 it was shorn of much of its elaborate finery, including the portico and tower, because of structural weakness.

WELLINGTON PUBLIC LIBRARY

In 1876 the Wellington Club trustees sold their Lambton Quay building to an ironmonger for £6,500 and bought an acre on the Terrace for £1,400. With the excess £5,100 they were well on the way to paying the contract price of £7,200 for the new clubhouse, shown in the photograph. It was designed by Thomas Turnbull in a style reminiscent of an Italian country house. Construction was preceded by extensive earthworks to level the site, shape the garden and channel the Kumutoto stream into a brick culvert. At the time of building, one of the Club's members, William Levin, was in England, and was given a budget of £1,000 to select suitable pictures, furniture and billiard tables for the premises.

The building was greatly added to over the years and was demolished in the early 1970s to make way for a new building, which has also since been demolished. The site is now occupied by one of the taller, finer modern office towers on the Terrace in which the Wellington Club has its own premises.

ALEXANDER TURNBULL LIBRARY

Throughout the world's major ports, institutions were set up for the welfare and entertainment of seafarers. Wellington was no exception with its Mission to Seamen. It was originally set up as a body of people who would arrange picnics for visiting seamen. However, a gift of money from Mary Anne Williams in memory of her late husband, Captain William Williams, meant that a building could be provided. Williams' gift of £7,000 was extremely generous, as was her offer to pay for all the furniture in the church room on the upper floor of the building. The Mission, on the corner of Stout and Ballance Streets, was designed by Crichton and McKay in 1903 and remains today one of the few Edwardian buildings in the city centre.
CANTERBURY TIMES

OPPOSITE

The Commercial Travellers and Warehousemen's Association had built clubrooms in Hunter Street just eight years before they decided to build new premises in Victoria Street — Wellington's warehouse golden mile. The photograph shows the Victoria Street building, designed in 1903 by Joshua Charlesworth in the Italian Renaissance style, which was noted for its controlled decoration and elegant proportions. (Charlesworth's other interesting work in this style is the Civil Service Club, which is still standing. It lies directly behind the old Public Trust building in Stout Street and is now incorporated into the new court building.) The Commercial Travellers building was constructed for £7,000. Its basement was used for cellarage and bicycle storage, the ground floor contained the bar and four sitting rooms, the first floor had the reading room along its entire frontage and a billiard room behind, and the top floor was left unfinished and available for rent.

The building later became the RSA headquarters but was demolished some time ago, along with the majority of contemporary buildings on Victoria Street.
HALL-RAINE COLLECTION, ALEXANDER TURNBULL LIBRARY

This photograph of Lambton Quay, taken about 1872, shows a survey party at work. Like other streets, the Quay had problems with dust and mud. Many schemes were suggested to have the mud scraped and collected by carts, but little lasting good came of this. To reduce the nuisance of dust, the City Council invited tenders for watering the streets. The watering was sporadic and irregular, even though a small dam was built at the top of Woodward Street where the carts could draw water. 'Apropos of dust,' demanded the *Evening Post* in February 1865, 'we should very much like to know whether the water cart proposition has been drowned in its infancy or what has become of it.'

At the extreme left of the photograph, and cut in half by the limits of the camera plate, are the premises of the Wellington Club before it was rebuilt on the Terrace in 1876. To the right of the clubhouse is one of the city's earliest decorated wooden commercial premises — Allan's pharmacy. It was built in 1869, and woodcuts were made of it to show the progress of the city in contemporary illustrated magazines.

The site photographed is now the Kingsway Development on the corner of the Quay and Bowen Street.

ALEXANDER TURNBULL LIBRARY

OPPOSITE

This photograph, taken in the mid-1880s, shows the suspension bridge over the gully which cut through Hobson Street. The bridge, built in 1878 by the City Council for £55, was a favourite playground for Thorndon youngsters. According to a published complaint in the *Evening Post* (October 1879), the game of making the bridge swing wildly while pedestrians were on it was not widely viewed as humorous. The gully was one of the city's many topographical challenges. It was suggested as a site for a rubbish dump as early as the 1870s. Although the suggestion was never officially sanctioned, the area was never 'beautified', and remained a wilderness for some decades.

On the right of the photograph is one of the city's grand architect-designed houses. It was built around 1882 for Henry Higginson, a railway engineer who had designed railway systems in England, Mauritius and Russia before coming to New Zealand. Higginson's house, with its other grand neighbours, led Hobson Street to be popularly termed 'Snobson Street'.

The site of this photograph is now the Hobson Street bridge over the motorway.

ALEXANDER TURNBULL LIBRARY

137

This view of the Terrace, taken about 1870, shows the state of most of Wellington's roads before surfacing was undertaken and footpaths formed. Primitive drainage can be seen in the form of a shallow brick channel running down the street and eventually ending up in the harbour by way of culverts, old stream beds or simple overflowing. In the early years prison labour was often used to form roads and make cuttings to reduce gradients. This photograph shows where a cutting was made in 1867, leaving many houses high above street level with their fences and gates hanging loose.

The state of the Terrace road was made even worse by herds of cattle being driven along it as an alternative route to the central city streets. On one occasion in February 1872 the *Evening Post* reported that 'ladies rushed frantically into houses and even men turned inside garden gates till the maddened brutes had torn past.'

ALEXANDER TURNBULL LIBRARY

OPPOSITE ABOVE

This photograph shows the Wellington City Tramways terminus buildings on Adelaide Road — a group of sheds built in 1877 housing the stables, carriages and engines. Work on laying the tracks started one morning in September 1877 with the workmen toasting the job ahead with a bottle of Hennessy cognac. Night shifts were sometimes needed to lay the tracks so as not to inconvenience daytime traffic. In August 1878 the first trip was made on a steam tram. A reckless 10 m.p.h. was achieved on the flat, and all the curves and gradients were negotiated with ease. As for the horses encountered along the way, few showed surprise, although one 'executed a polka, arranged as a solo for four feet . . . perhaps this is because the cars are painted a glaring scarlet picked out with gold.' The public was given eight hours' free travel on opening day. The offer was so enthusiastically taken up by school children in the late afternoon that by 8 p.m. they were all told to go home. At first the trams ran every half hour, but the frequency was increased as more engines arrived from England. An average of 2,500 used the trams each day. It was obviously a well-patronised enterprise, even if there were to be financial defeats ahead. By 1882 the steam engines were

dispensed with because of their expense and cumbersome nature, and the Tramway Company changed to horse power. Vast stables were added to the Newtown terminus with accommodation for fifty horses. The trams ran on horse power until electrification at the turn of the century.
GORDON BURT COLLECTION, ALEXANDER TURNBULL LIBRARY

One of the largest streetworks in Wellington was the electrification of the trams, which began in 1903 with the building of a £20,000 powerhouse opposite the new Town Hall. The old rails were then lifted, the entire road crown removed, new rails, poles and wires laid and the road resurfaced with wooden blocks. The work required an army of labourers, often operating nightshifts. The poles for the overhead wires were ironbark imported from Australia at £5 each — about half the cost of similar poles made from local totara. The poles were also to carry the city's electricity and telephone wires, adding to the intricacy and scope of the job.

The photograph at right shows new rails and switches being laid at the corner of Manners and Cuba Streets.
ALEXANDER TURNBULL LIBRARY

140

OPPOSITE

Another private transport venture that was subsequently corporatised was the Kelburn Cable Car, or the High Levels Tramway as it was originally termed. By 1898 most of the money required had been subscribed to the syndicate who proposed the venture, a venture which went hand in hand with the surveying of the forty-nine hectares of the Upland Farm to become the suburb of Kelburn. After the necessary government moves to take land for the tunnels and viaducts had been accomplished, work began in late 1899 by contractor Maurice O'Connor for a price close to £12,000. The directors called on Frederick Clere to design a three-storeyed, French-styled building as office premises on Lambton Quay at the entrance to the cable car terminus. It is one of the few late nineteenth-century buildings remaining along this street. Work on the cable car was sporadically hampered by some property owners laying claim for damage and by a few slips in the tunnels. The cables and rails were late to arrive from England, causing a further delay. There was a debate over the traction power to be used, but by early 1902 the cable car was running. The service originally ran until 11 p.m. each week night, and such was the initial novelty that about 1,500 people used it each day for some time following its opening. The Tramway Company later leased land from the City Council at the top of the incline and had John Swan design the tea house in the photograph, more widely known as the Kelburn Kiosk. It was built in record time (about 15 weeks) by contractor J. H. Meyer for £2,300 and for decades was one of the city's best known and widely used recreation spots.

ALEXANDER TURNBULL LIBRARY

This placid view over the Thorndon foreshore shows the Wellington Railway Station, built in 1880 to designs by local engineer John Blackett to replace a small shed further along towards Pipitea Point. Its construction in wood was seen as a deliberate slight to the city, as wood had already been outlawed as a building material in the central area. A deputation went to the government and was told that the station was to be of wood or nothing at all, and that priority was to be given to line construction rather than station building. The deputation was also told that the building was intended to be temporary. In fact, it stood for over fifty years.

The *New Zealand Mail* was shown plans for the station, and reported, 'we must confess to a feeling of disappointment at the size and character of the building, but admit that it will be infinitely superior to the present structure at Pipitea Point, and are prepared to be thankful for small mercies' (April 1880). However, the *Evening Post* was cynical when it saw the designs for the goods sheds built nearby soon after: '[if they are to be] as imposing in their architectural character as the passenger station, they will be a magnificent ornament to this city' (October 1880).

Visible behind the station are a number of vessels moored at the railway wharf.

ALEXANDER TURNBULL LIBRARY

The first electric light standard erected in Wellington is shown in this view of Lambton Quay. It was a gift from the Mayor, Samuel Brown, to the city in 1888 as an expression of his faith in the marvel of electric lighting. A year earlier the city had been given a public display of electricity with a number of powerful spotlights, and within a few months the City Council invited tenders for 450 lamps in Paris, London and New York. The contract was won by the Gülcher Company of London, who sent out all the wiring, lights and dynamos required. However, the Council had to supply the water to the two dynamo stations in Featherston and Manners Streets. The electric lights cost about £3 each compared with £9 for each gas lamp, and had a candle-power of twenty, compared with fourteen for gas. At first 500 lights were installed around the central city and were kept on from dusk until dawn. The efficiency of electric power was quickly recognised, and the lighting was soon extended throughout the city.
AUTHOR

OPPOSITE

This photograph of the Te Aro foreshore, taken about 1883, shows the enormous gasometer and coal shed of the Wellington Gas Company in the centre. The site is now the middle of Courtenay Place. The building was completed in 1878. All the castings were done in London and specially strengthened to withstand the Wellington winds, then shipped to New Zealand. Gas was first used to light the city one Saturday night in April 1871 when all the standards which had been imported from Glasgow were illuminated. The gas took about four hours to push all the air out of the pipes along Lambton Quay. Later gas lighting and heating were used in virtually every public building and quite a few houses, and were the cause of some destructive fires.

The photograph also shows the trestle railway used to cart spoil from the quarries at Oriental Bay to the extensive reclamations of the Te Aro foreshore.
AUTHOR

This view over Bolton Street Cemetery towards Hill Street, taken about 1890, shows how overgrown the area was. Public outrage about the conditions and hazards of Bolton Street was fierce before the new cemetery opened in Karori. In August 1880 the *New Zealand Mail* ran a piece about the reckless manner of interment in the cemetery, which consisted mainly of slippery clay slopes accessible only by steep paths and cuttings: 'human corruption is continually bubbling out and trickling down,' it stated.

Two years later it reported renewed complaints about the repulsive odours and sent the Council's Inspector of Nuisances to investigate. An area of ground, it was noted with some distaste, had already been used three times for burial, and a child's coffin was lying about with part of the lid gone 'but portions of the cloth still adhering and fluttering in the wind.'

ALEXANDER TURNBULL LIBRARY

This is the Wellington Telephone Exchange, built in 1883 in Stout Street and opened with thirty-six subscribers. The first telephone in the city was rigged up by ironmonger Edward Mills in 1878 from his Hunter Street office to his warehouse on Featherston Street and then to his foundry in Customhouse Quay. The 550 metres of wires needed were simply slung across the rooftops along the way. Others followed Mills's initiative and soon a central exchange was needed. Although it was an expensive service (a £12 initial fee was charged, and calls cost 6d each), it soon attracted a number of private subscribers who had their houses fitted with telephones. As an added service, the exchange was kept open until 2 a.m. each day. Wall sheets were printed and circulated to keep subscribers informed of new numbers, and the newspapers regularly carried lists of new subscribers. In 1906 the first proper telephone directory was published in Wellington, a ninety-page book listing 2,400 numbers. It was widely acclaimed as it replaced the loose wall sheets which had 'hung in dog-eared condition on a nail — when a nail happened to be there' (*Evening Post*, June 1906).

ALEXANDER TURNBULL LIBRARY

Everyone viewed fire with alarm in colonial Wellington, yet provision for organised fire fighting was slow to get underway. The first volunteer force, the Wellington Brigade, was not formed until 1865. Two years later a splinter group, the Central Brigade, came into existence. The City Council, insurance companies, and business owners were so enthusiastic about these brigades that they made generous donations of machinery and money. Both brigades worked from separate stations — the Central from Brandon Street and the Wellington from Manners Street. A centrally located fire station was finally built in 1901.

This photograph shows the ceremony for laying the foundation stone. The premises were situated opposite what was to be the Town Hall. The building was designed by the City Engineer and had a large machine room, loose-boxes for the horses, accommodation for fifteen firefighters, a recreation hall and also a Superintendent's residence. It did service to the city until the opening of the present Central Fire Station on Clyde Quay in 1938, and was finally demolished in 1957.

Horse transport was used for many years, and even after the brigade acquired its first motor appliance in 1906, horses were kept until 1913. This photograph shows some of the well-conditioned horses and the much-admired uniforms of the men. In the background is one of the city's band rotundas, which was built in 1898 to designs by George Schwartz. Its position soon became unattractive because of the noise of the trams, the fire station, the wharves and general bustle of the area.

WELLINGTON PUBLIC LIBRARY

This photograph of the Te Aro flat, taken in 1858, shows Wellington before it became the capital — a small wooden town without the financial backing from agriculture, mineral extraction, manufacturing or Custom's receipts. This is Wellington with a population of about 4,000, where the thought of suburbs was decades away and even Oriental Bay, visible here as a series of steep headlands, was all but *ultima Thule*. The photograph was taken three years after the severe earthquake of 1855, which led many people to abandon the settlement. However, the earthquake lifted the land at Te Aro sufficiently high to help it lose the stigma of a swamp overgrown with towering flax bushes.

In the middle of the photograph (on the corner of Willis and Ghuznee Streets) is St Peter's Anglican church, with additions to its 1848 nucleus. Barely discernible in the main gable head is the first of the city's town clocks, brought from England by a returning colonist.

ALEXANDER TURNBULL LIBRARY

The pioneer wooden cottages of Wellington are beautifully illustrated in this photograph of Cuba Street, taken in 1864. They were built close to the footpath, and shingles were the dominant roofing material. Most cottages had a centrally located door and rooms on either side. Palings were the popular fencing. The cottage on the left with the ornate sign on the roof was the house and factory of Edward Dixon, a ginger beer manufacturer. The youth leaning on his rifle in front of the fence is a reminder of the military presence in Wellington. A militia was originally formed in readiness for Maori war parties, and later was incorporated into a countrywide defence force under the aegis of central government.
ALEXANDER TURNBULL LIBRARY

OPPOSITE

The two characteristics of Thorndon — the large estate, and the densely built streets — are clearly visible in this photograph, taken about 1880. Hobson Street and Fitzherbert Terrace are on the left of the Thorndon flat. Here were built some of the houses of the city's merchants, with large gardens and views over the foreshore. (Note the prominent observation tower on T. C. Williams' house in Hobson Street, now part of Queen Margaret College.)

To the right of the flat is the densely built area around Molesworth and Mulgrave Streets, which was renowned in the 1870s for its overcrowding, narrow streets, disturbances and brothels.
AUTHOR

ABOVE

This view of the slopes of Mt Victoria, taken about 1885, shows part of the suburb's rather genteel development. Close subdivision of town acres and estates was still a few decades away, and the suburb's views were not yet obliterated by high rise on the Te Aro flat. Taken from one corner of the Basin Reserve, the photograph has captured in the foreground some of the pine tree borders of the reserve. The trees and extensive drainage did much to change the Basin from a swamp to a popular public park.

Along the middle of the photograph runs Kent Terrace which, with Cambridge Terrace, formed a clear distinction between the flat and the slopes. Kent Terrace already has a number of buildings on it, predominantly boarding houses and private hotels.

The arrowed building is one of Mt Victoria's grander private houses on Brougham Street. Known as 'Brougham Bank', it is still standing, although in vastly altered form. It was built on two acres in 1877 for ironmonger William Dawson, and contained fifteen rooms. In 1889 it was bought by Justice Richmond, who renamed it 'Windhover'.

The naming of houses was a regular practice in colonial New Zealand. They were named after families, English place names, the topography, Maori associations and suchlike. Other Mt Victoria named houses of note included: J. E. FitzGerald's 'Clyde Cliff' in Hawker Street; G. W. Aitken's 'Echobank' in Hawker Street; James Sloan's 'Nithbank' in Majoribanks Street; R. C. Hamerton's 'The Holies' in Austin Street; W. H. Atack's 'Dorset House' in Pirie Street; and Alex Veitch's 'Wairenga' in Claremont Grove.

BURTON BROTHERS COLLECTION, ALEXANDER TURNBULL LIBRARY

BELOW

This photograph of Oriental Bay, taken about 1885, shows some of the elegant 'marine villas' along the Parade. It was taken at low tide before sea walls were built and the road widened. At the left are three of a group of five similarly styled houses built for leasing in the early 1880s. In the middle (on the corner of present-day Grass Street) is the house built in 1877 for William Hales, Engineer-in-Chief for the colony. He married Catherine Wilkinson whose father, David Wilkinson, ran the pleasure gardens further up Grass Street. Next along the Parade towards town is the solid-looking house built in 1878 for R. C. Shearman, the first Chief-of-Police who had arrived in New Zealand with the colony's first Governor, William Hobson.

Behind the houses the deforested hills rise sharply, accessible only by a few goat tracks. Land was soon in great demand, and by the turn of the century these hills hosted a cluster of houses connected by precipitous streets and narrow rights-of-way.

Oriental Parade was formerly known as O'Neill's Esplanade after the engineer Charles O'Neill who put it through. In the late 1870s it was widened considerably, making the area more suitable for house sites. The Council was determined that the shoreline should not be reclaimed or built on. When the tram lines were put through and Roseneath opened up, the Parade underwent much improvement. As the *Evening Post* said in April 1908, '[the work was] designed to make the old-boot and tin-can depot a beautiful promenade.'

ELLIS COLLECTION, ALEXANDER TURNBULL LIBRARY

The full extent of close subdivision and dense housing on the Te Aro flat can be seen in this photograph, taken in 1905. The houses were built almost entirely in wood and were of a distinctly better quality than the speculative houses of the 1870s. The standards of servicing, such as drainage, road widths and water supply, were well enforced by City Council bylaws and inspectors. The dense building resulted in a number of small streets, although many of these have since been obliterated.

The domestic nature of the area has been radically altered over the years by the encroachment from industry and commerce, and by street alignment and the motorway.
AUTHOR

OPPOSITE

The suburb of Newtown had been planned from the early days of Wellington. Its land was divided into town acres on the original maps, and its main streets were named. Some land speculators might have hoped for healthy profits from a boom in demand. However, it was not until the 1890s when the rate of house building increased that a substantial number of large holdings were cut up. Connecting streets were put through and architects were called upon to design groups of similarly styled houses for clients as investments. The row of twelve double-storeyed villas along Russell Terrace in the foreground were all designed by James O'Dea in 1901 for landed gentleman and hotel owner Hamilton Gilmer.

Also prominent, left of centre, is one of the city's brick-making works. This and other local industries allowed Newtown to grow in its own right as a 'village' and as a suburb of central Wellington. Other features that helped Newtown become virtually self-sufficient were its churches, schools, recreation amenities and the ribbon development of shops along the main thoroughfares.

This photograph was taken in 1908 when Wellington's population was around 65,000 and the suburbs of Roseneath, Hataitai, Kilbirnie, Brooklyn, Kelburn and Karori were well established.
S. C. SMITH COLLECTION, ALEXANDER TURNBULL LIBRARY

The Hutt Valley was intended as the original site for Wellington. However, within months of landfall the colonists moved the seat of the city across the harbour. This left the Hutt somewhat bereft of development. Episodes of war with the Maori, the difficult river and the large percentage of absentee landowning meant the area was neglected for some time. It was divided into about eighty sections, each of about eighty hectares. The Hutt did have a village nucleus, which can be seen in this photograph, taken in the mid-1880s. By this time, the Hutt Valley had numerous farms (mostly for grazing, although there was appreciable cropping), some elegant estates, and a serenity that was to be short-lived. Several factors contributed to the Hutt's development as a settlement: the railway line through the valley to Wairarapa; the introduction of some large industry at Petone (Railways workshops in 1877, Gear Meat in 1883 and the Wellington Woollen Company in 1884); the confining of the Hutt River by stopbanks; and land subdivision fuelled by high rating on unimproved land.

The Hutt township had a population of about 1,500 at the time of the photograph. To the right can be seen the fourth bridge to be built across the river, constructed of totara spans in 1872. In the centre of the town is St James's Anglican Church, designed by Thomas Turnbull in 1879 and destroyed by fire in 1946.

ALEXANDER TURNBULL LIBRARY

This unfocused snapshot, taken in 1903, shows one of Wellington's well-known medics, Dr William Chapple, with his wife and daughter in their newly imported motorcar outside their 'San Francisco'-styled house on the corner of Willis and Dixon Streets. The car is little more than a motorised buggy, steered by a handlebar rather than a wheel, and chain driven. It was not long before larger cars with covered bodies, chauffeurs' seats and greater horsepower became available.

'Motor cars are rapidly increasing in number in Wellington,' the *Weekly Press* reported in May 1903, but 'a very objectionable feature developed by cars is that of getting puffed, just like a human being when there is a rise to ascend. When a hill appears in view it is no unusual thing to see the occupants of a motor tipped out on the roadside whilst the driver ascends in lonely state.'

NEW ZEALAND GRAPHIC

The Hon John Johnston's house in Fitzherbert Terrace shows the architecture of Thomas Turnbull at its most formal and imposing. The house went up in 1875, when Johnston himself was sixty-six years old and his eldest child was twenty-one. Johnston's unmarried daughter, Emily, inherited the house on his death in 1887. Her lavish entertainments were fully written up in the social columns of the press.

Her party-giving was noted for its variety and included the famous evening garden parties, fancy-dress parties, 'at homes' to meet officers from visiting warships in port, theme dances, charity garden parties, children's parties with decorated go-carts and perambulators, and fortune-telling sessions. One of the latter, held in September 1892, was described by the *New Zealand Graphic*; 'upon entering the witches' uncanny presence one saw the fortune teller crouching on the floor in Eastern dress, her hair streamy and half veiled and her coloured face gleaming in the dim lights. She was surrounded by a huge bowl, some fish bones and other extraordinary things, besides a vast amount of flame and smoke.'

The Johnston residence was demolished in the mid-1930s and the site is now the tennis courts off Katherine Avenue.

ELLIS COLLECTION, ALEXANDER TURNBULL LIBRARY

'Moana Lua', built for Robert Levin in 1902, was designed by John Swan in a style that suggested a cosy castle. Constructed in reinforced concrete and smothered with plaster decoration, the house was a marvel not only of modern interior decoration but also of modern conveniences. Particularly notable was the house's complete heating by steam radiators, the boilers for which were placed in the basement, and the flues in the vast attic space. All the lighting was electricity and included a 'burglar switch', which would light up every corridor in the house when pressed. The internal system of 'telephonettes' was another modern convenience that enabled people to talk to each other from one room to another.

'Moana Lua' was demolished in 1975 and the site is now occupied by the Australian High Commission.
AUTHOR

OPPOSITE

This view of a portion of Hobson Street shows two of the grander houses of colonial Wellington. On the left is the decorated residence of Jacob Joseph, designed in 1877 by Thomas Turnbull, the architect for many of Joseph's investment and commercial buildings in the city. On the right is 'Edendale House', originally built for Robert Stains, whose partner, John Kirkcaldie, lived at 'Kinnoul', high up on Thompson Street on the other side of the city.

Both these houses were demolished some time ago, and their sites now form part of the Wellington Girls' College playing grounds.
ELLIS COLLECTION, ALEXANDER TURNBULL LIBRARY

Although central city space was at a premium at the turn of the century, it did not deter some of the wealthy from building homes there. This glorious piece of French Renaissance-styled design was produced in 1905 by Crichton and McKay for dentist Henry Rawson, at a cost of over £6,000, on the corner of the Terrace and Woodward Street. The two lower floors formed by the sloping site were professional offices — the ground floor for Charles Turner, dermatologist, and the first floor shared by Rawson and Dr Garcia Webster. Above this, with its main entrance on the Terrace, was the fourteen-roomed residence of Henry Rawson. It was built in brick, with a double-height entrance hall. All the partitions inside had asbestos lining for fireproofing, and the house was also fitted with fire escapes, worked into the design. The wood used for framing was jarrah and the interior woodwork was oiled red pine. The house also had a large flat roof, which was used as a promenade with views over the harbour.

AUTHOR

Saunders Lane (now Little George Street), off Tinakori Road, Thorndon, was one of the city's numerous private lanes. It was owned by well-known contractor Joseph Saunders and consisted of eight four-roomed cottages of minimal quality and finish. It ran through a natural hollow and this photograph, taken after one of the city's most disastrous floods in 1891, shows how vulnerable the houses were to the flood. It also shows a density of housing that was widely attributed to a greed for land and a surge in population caused by immigration.

To the left on the skyline just across Tinakori Road is the big house 'Lednam' (formed from the name of one-time owner, Joseph Mandel, spelled backwards). At the time, it was owned by the director of the BNZ, Harold Beauchamp. His daughter, Katherine Mansfield, was later to use this house and the little hovels of Saunders Lane as the setting for her short story 'The Garden Party'.

ALEXANDER TURNBULL LIBRARY

This photograph of the Albion Hotel on Molesworth Street, Thorndon, also shows a section of the narrow, unformed Fraser's Lane (now Aitken Street), one of the city's many slum streets. Fraser's Lane (only three metres wide) and its adjoining Wingfield and John Streets were sporadically in the press as the location of a number of brothels. The hot-blooded disturbances, thefts and fights in these areas often ended up on the magistrate's charge sheets. In 1882 two children aged five and seven appeared before the magistrate on charges of being neglected children whose mother ran a brothel in Wingfield Street. They were sent to the industrial schools for seven years. In 1885 five prostitutes from Fraser's Lane went to Philomene McHugh's brothel in Wingfield Street and a battle ensued, ending up in court. In 1886 two prostitutes, Nellie Hamilton and Elizabeth Brighting, were convicted of being noisy and were each sentenced to seven days' imprisonment, with fines. In 1894 the Disorderly House Bylaw (prohibiting brothels in the city) was used for the first time against five women running brothels in John Street. They were discharged with a caution, even though the law allowed for a £5 fine with £5 for each subsequent offending day.

The site of this photograph is now the National Library.

ALEXANDER TURNBULL LIBRARY

In 1905 Lionel Terry, pamphleteer, traveller, anti-Chinese *agent provocateur* and general xenophobe, shot an old Chinese man dead in Haining Street as an expression of his extreme views of racial purity. Terry quickly gave himself up, and the resulting murder trial was avidly followed by the press — Terry was to spend the rest of his life in lunatic asylums. This press photograph shows Haining Street within days of the shooting.

The street was frequently cited as an example of slum housing. Views of its backyards were even used as lantern slide illustrations for public lectures on slums, which did a countrywide tour about the same time as Terry's act of murder. Billed as 'the most notorious slum quarter in New Zealand' (*Auckland Weekly News*, September 1911), it was planned to be removed in a clean-up scheme for the Te Aro basin, mooted in 1911. It was to have been replaced by wider streets, new buildings and grassed squares. Nothing happened, and the street still exists, although no trace of its squalid past remains.

AUCKLAND WEEKLY NEWS

ABOVE

In 1882 an anonymous pledge of £1,000 was made to build a home for Wellington's destitute people, if the City Council provided the site. The Council invited tenders for a site, the government offered a handsome subsidy and by 1886 a design competition for the institution was held for the agreed site at the rear of the public hospital. The competition was won by Joshua Charlesworth, whose design, illustrated, provided accommodation for sixty people. Built in 1888 for £3,000, at first it comprised just one wing for men and the central administration block with an apartment for the Superintendent. By 1898 the other wing was built and the institution was supported by boarding charges, government aid and ongoing donations from the public. This building (then called the Home for the Aged Needy) has since been demolished. However, the institution now known as the Te Hopai Home remains on its original site.

WELLINGTON PUBLIC LIBRARY

BELOW

The call on public money to fund projects in colonial New Zealand was widespread, incessant, and often the reason behind large garden fêtes. As part of the fundraising for the Veterans' Home, a fête was held in the gardens of Government House in October 1904, organised by Lady Plunket, wife of the colony's Governor. This photograph shows Lady Plunket's three daughters in attendance at the bran tub. The fête also included a 'treasure dig' in a bed of soil near the vegetable garden, which may not have greatly tempted the many society ladies present in their stylish afternoon tea gowns. The fête was judged a success by the press and the proceeds augmented the fund. The Veterans' Home was built in Auckland as a home for old and penurious war veterans. It was designed by the Wellington architect E. W. G. Coleridge, who waived his fees as his contribution.

NEW ZEALAND GRAPHIC

161

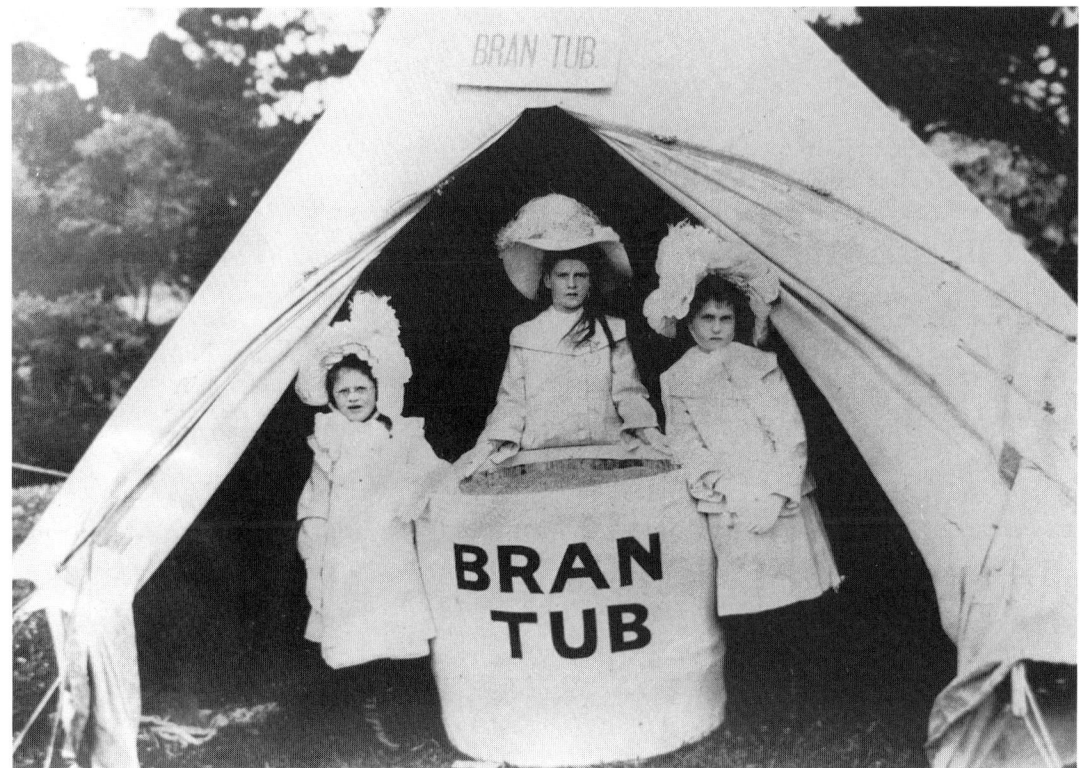

This photograph shows the orphan girls of the Salvation Army's Pauline Home setting out for a picnic in the Akatarawa Hills one day in March 1913. The cars were lent by members of the public and the picnic lunch was provided by the city's foremost private caterer, James Godber of Cuba Street.

The Pauline Home was built at the top of Owen Street, Newtown, in 1907. The existence of such a home illustrates the practical concern for the plight of orphans at the time. It was not the city's only orphanage. Within a stone's throw was the Army's 'Rescue Home' for young women ensnared in virtual child prostitution. Another Salvation Army home in colonial Wellington was the Maternity Home in Ellice Street for unmarried mothers having their first babies — 'second offences' were not admitted.

Even before Wellington became the capital, the perceived need for institutions was publicly discussed. In 1864 plans were drawn up for a self-supporting 'Magdalen Asylum' to accommodate a matron and ten inmates — '[those] unhappy female outcasts who nightly wander through our streets' (*Wellington Independent*, March 1864).
WEEKLY PRESS

OPPOSITE

Scattered throughout central Wellington were boarding houses, home to many tradesmen and labourers. The boarding houses were often run by professional women for whom it might provide a living. This photograph shows one such establishment in Willis Street, a few doors up from Boulcott Street. A dingy looking place, it typifies much of the central city semi-domestic architecture of the 1880s, decorated on the street face with very ordinary kit-set embellishments like verandah brackets and lathed balusters, but behind this, a maze of substandard rooms with little natural light. The nine men on the verandah were presumably boarders.

Wellington had better and worse boarding houses than this. Top of the range was Miss Malcolm's at 114 the Terrace. She welcomed Members of Parliament (who used it for sessional accommodation) and the visiting well-heeled such as judges, bank inspectors, merchants and run-holders. Her steep tariff of £5 a week was about double that charged by the leading hotels of the city.
S. C. SMITH COLLECTION, ALEXANDER TURNBULL LIBRARY

FISH & CHIP SUPPERS 6d

GRAND OYSTER SALOON

FISH & CHIPS

FISH SUPPERS

FISH & CHIPS TO TAKE HOME

L. DRISCOLL,
BUILDER & CONTRACTOR
SHOP & OFFICE FITTER
Jobbing Work of every description.
Estimates Free.

BOARD AND RESIDENCE 17/- week
BOARD 12/6 ALL MEALS 9d
Mrs A. Walls, Proprietress.

STABLES TOILET

164

OPPOSITE

St Andrew's Presbyterian Church was designed by Christian Toxward in 1878 to replace the church on Lambton Quay, which was sold to the Colonial Bank. It was one of the country's first churches inspired by the Classical style. The tower was topped off by a gilded sphere and could be seen from some distance. Its interior was a large, single volume with gallery seating along the sides supported on carved columns. All the seats were upholstered in velvet, the doors were padded with crimson cloth and the woodwork was fashioned from Singapore cedar. It had a notable airiness and excellent natural lighting from rows of windows along the side walls. The £4,000 it cost to build was considered money well spent. It had such strong architectural merits that the new church built on this site in 1919 closely followed the stylistic lines of Toxward's building, although this time concrete was used for construction, not wood.

ALEXANDER TURNBULL LIBRARY

This photograph of Lambton Quay shows a portion of the damage from the fire of 1906. Vast showers of cinders had landed on roofs for some distance and much effort was needed to dampen down threatened buildings. When the Union Bank caught fire, the stiff wind spread thousands of bank receipts all over the city. The heat from the blaze also fused tram and electricity wires, and much of the wood-blocking used to pave the streets had also caught fire and was badly charred.

The photograph is taken from the rubble of Grey Street some weeks after the blaze. At the right is the Trocadero Private Hotel with its facade in scaffolding. One hundred and sixty guests were evacuated from the hotel during the fire. To the left of this is a hurriedly rebuilt Commercial Hotel. The original three-storeyed wooden building of 1877 had gone up in flames in a matter of minutes. Across a litter-strewn section stands the burnt-out shell of the Bank of New South Wales, which had been open for business for barely a year.

On the skyline, built on a tongue of land jutting out from the Terrace, stands the undamaged house of William Field, MP, built in 1898 to designs by Clere, FitzGerald and Richmond.

NEW ZEALAND GRAPHIC

OPPOSITE

The wooden Parliament Buildings were destroyed by fire early in the morning of Wednesday 11 December 1907. The fire raged for six hours and left the area looking like the 'dregs of a furnace'. It was discovered at 2 a.m. by the night watchman, who raised the alarm. However, the fire spread so rapidly that much energy was spent salvaging records and dampening down the brick General Assembly Library. By 3 a.m. smoke was pouring from the building 'like volumes of blood-red steam'. Police roped off the area and thousands of people came to watch. The *Evening Post* reported, '[the light of the fire] lit up a weird army, which had come out in dressing-gowns and overcoats . . . the flames gobbled up a turret, and reached out for other delicacies . . . The flames were firing salutes in honour of themselves . . . the blackbirds and thrushes began to sing to their mates. The business of the rest of the world was going on as usual.'

After the fire the Governor vacated Government House, which was used as a temporary Parliament. It was connected to the General Assembly Library by an extraordinary elevated corridor about sixty metres long. In 1911 a design competition was held for a new Parliament Building. It was won by John Campbell, but construction was slow to begin. When the building opened in 1918 less than half of Campbell's design had been built. It was not until the late 1960s, with the Beehive's construction, that significant accommodation was added for the workings of government.

ALEXANDER TURNBULL LIBRARY

After the Parliament Buildings were burned down, the Governor, Lord Plunket, vacated his official residence and took a two-year lease on John Strang's peaceful house 'Woodhey', sited in large grounds close to a boating lagoon at Hokowhitu, Palmerston North. Workmen then moved into Government House and considerably altered its interior to suit the needs of Parliament. Work was also soon to begin on the present Government House near the Basin Reserve. In this photograph builders are turning the reception rooms of the house into a debating chamber for the House of Representatives.

During their stay in Wellington the Plunkets held many functions and balls in these rooms. In July 1904 the social columnist for the *Weekly Press* lamented that the balls started as late as 10 p.m.: 'Of course that is the usual time in London, but out here, in this less sophisticated land, half of us are in bed by that time.'

NEW ZEALAND GRAPHIC

THE NATIONAL DAIRY ASSOCIATION OF N.Z. WELCOMES THE DUKE & DUCHESS OF CORNWALL & YORK

OPPOSITE

This festive photograph of Lambton Quay shows one of the six arches built along the route from Queen's Wharf to Government House for the Royal Visit of 1901. The arch was built by the National Dairy Association and designed by Edward Blake. It was made from butter-box heads and cheese crates and called the Butter Arch. Also adorning the route were the Citizens Arch, the Wellington Woollen Company Arch (with the motto 'See the warmth of our welcome'), the Foreign Consuls Arch, the Chinese Arch and finally the Government Arch with its valuable Maori carvings from the collections of the Colonial Museum and bibliophile Alexander Turnbull. These arches were only finished on the eve of the royal party's arrival in Wellington. The royal route was lined with hundreds of brightly coloured flags and Venetian masts. The people of Wellington turned out to welcome the royal visitors, and many balconies were leased for the best view. After the festivities the arches were auctioned for their materials.

McALLISTER COLLECTION, ALEXANDER TURNBULL LIBRARY

For as long as Wellington had been a European settlement, Queen Victoria had been the British Empire's sovereign, and her position as political and social figurehead was unquestioned. When Victoria celebrated her Diamond Jubilee in 1897 Wellington marked the occasion by commissioning a jubilee sculpture of the monarch. Paid for by public donation, the bronze figure was cast by English sculptor Alfred Drury, who sent out a model which was exhibited in the window of McGregor Wright's art gallery. The Queen's Statue Committee duly authorised the work, which cost about £1,850 and was to be paid for in four instalments. The first sections of the sculpture arrived in Wellington early in 1905 (eight years after the jubilee and three years after the monarch's death) and the work was soon a fixture at the entrance to Queen's Wharf. In 1911 the statue and its enormous base were shifted to the garden strip separating Kent and Cambridge Terraces. The move became necessary because of increased traffic around Queen's Wharf and the laying of electric tramlines through the area. The photograph shows the statue being lowered before being taken to its more sylvan and peaceful setting.

NEW ZEALAND GRAPHIC

Part of the public send-off of the Second Contingent to the Boer War in South Africa is shown in this photograph, taken in January 1900. The structure to the left on the waterfront, with its decorative half-timbering and observation tower, was designed in 1894 by Frederick Clere for the Wellington Naval Artillery. This was one of many local militia groups set up throughout the country to provide a defence network. Its formation was prompted by a Russian warship scare in the 1880s, which also resulted in the establishment of forts and gun emplacements around the country's major harbours.

The building to the right is the premises of the Star Boating Club, which had been formed in 1866. This building was designed by William Chatfield in 1886 and built for £1,500 at the bottom of Harbour Street (now Willeston Street). The building was designed to be moved without difficulty after harbour reclamation. Three years later it was shifted to the site shown here. The 100-tonne building was hoisted onto twenty-five railway bogeys and hauled along specially laid tram tracks.

Both sheds have recently been resited as part of the Lambton Harbour redevelopment.

WELLINGTON PUBLIC LIBRARY

This photograph of Lambton Quay, now the site of the old Public Trust building, shows the exhibition hall built for Wellington's first Industrial Exhibition in 1885. Exhibitions were held regularly through the British Empire and provided an opportunity for manufacturers to show off wares such as stationery, glassware, ironmongery, furnishings, jewellery and food to an appreciative public. The buildings, which were only temporary, were designed by engineer John Blackett. The framing was made of railway iron, the wood was second-class rimu, the sheathing was corrugated iron and the windows were calico. The building was far advanced in early 1885 when most of it was destroyed in a gale. Inspection showed the construction was feeble and without foundations. It was quickly rebuilt and the show opened in August, even though the catalogues, which had been printed in Dunedin, failed to arrive in time. Open for thirteen weeks, the exhibition was attended by thousands of people, bringing hundreds of tourist pounds to the city. Afterwards many of the exhibits were sent on to London for the Indian and Colonial Exhibition, and the buildings on the corner of the Quay and Stout Street were demolished for the second time.

ALEXANDER TURNBULL LIBRARY

KEY TO MAP

Key to buildings identified on the map on pages 174–175, which is based on a turn-of-the-century street map of Wellington.

1. Dr Harding's house and surgery
2. First Union Bank, later the Albert Hotel
3. Public Library
4. Town Hall
5. Fire Station
6. St Mary of the Angels
7. Oriental Hotel
8. Grand Hotel
9. Roman Catholic Boys' School
10. King's Chambers
11. CML
12. Commercial Travellers' Club
13. BNZ
14. Athenaeum
15. St Andrew's, Lambton Quay
16. Central Hotel
17. NMLA
18. Supreme Court, later Bank of New South Wales
19. Union Bank
20. Bannatyne warehouse
21. AMP
22. NZI
23. Nathan's warehouse
24. Cable Car Lane buildings
25. Oddfellows' Hall
26. National Bank
27. Dawson's ironmongery
28. Post Office
29. Wellington College, later Clifton Terrace School
30. Synagogue
31. City Corporation buildings
32. Wellington Provincial Council Chambers, later Government Life
33. Kirkcaldie and Stains
34. Kirkcaldie and Stains middle block
35. W. and G. Turnbull warehouse
36. Occidental Hotel
37. Theatre Royal
38. Wellington Club
39. J. Joseph warehouse
40. Public Trust
41. Mission to Seamen
42. St Andrew's, The Terrace
43. Supreme Court
44. Gear Meat
45. Scoullar warehouse
46. Government departmental buildings
47. Congregational Church
48. Museum
49. Government House
50. Parliament
51. General Assembly Library
52. St Mary's, Hill Street

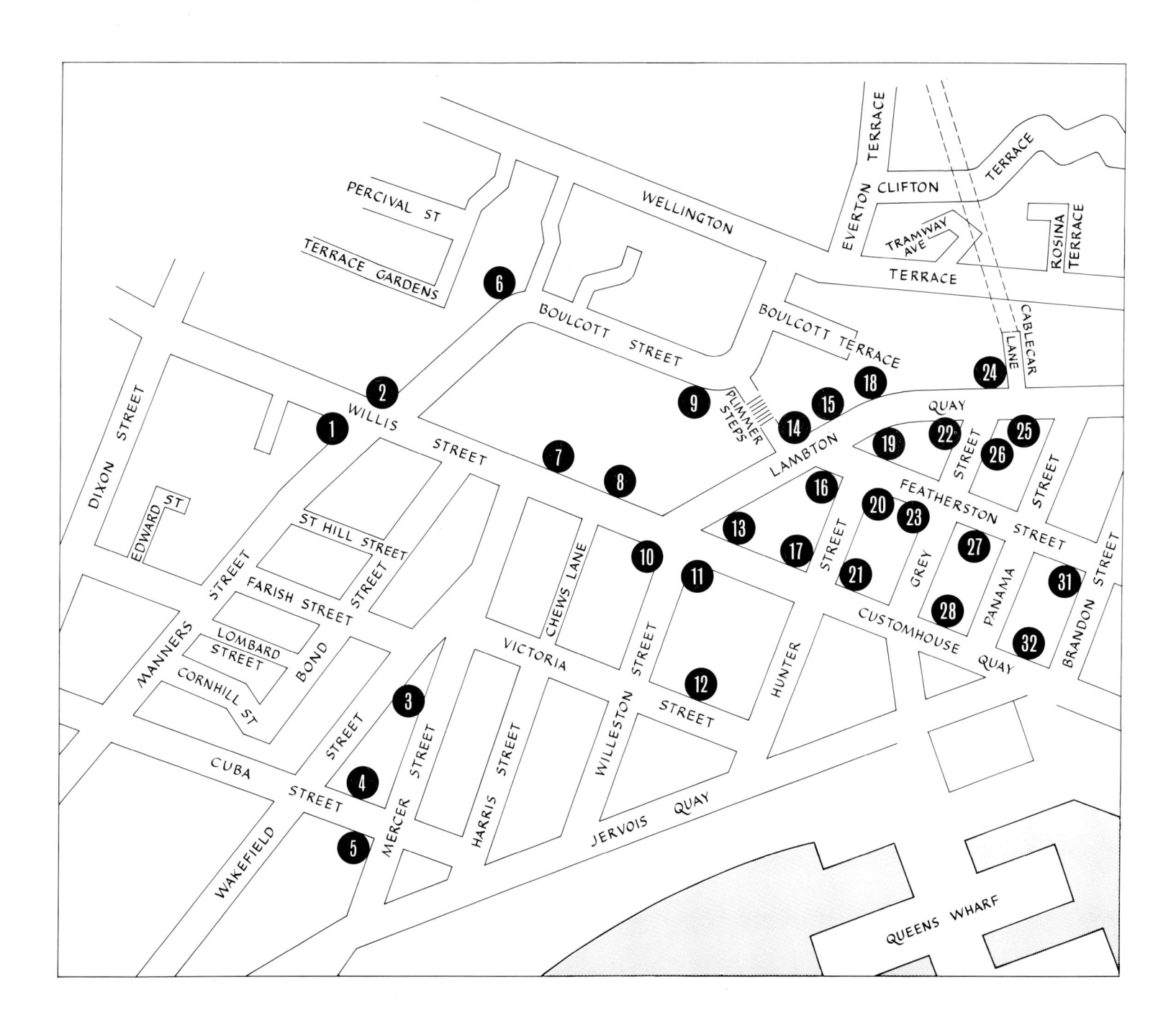

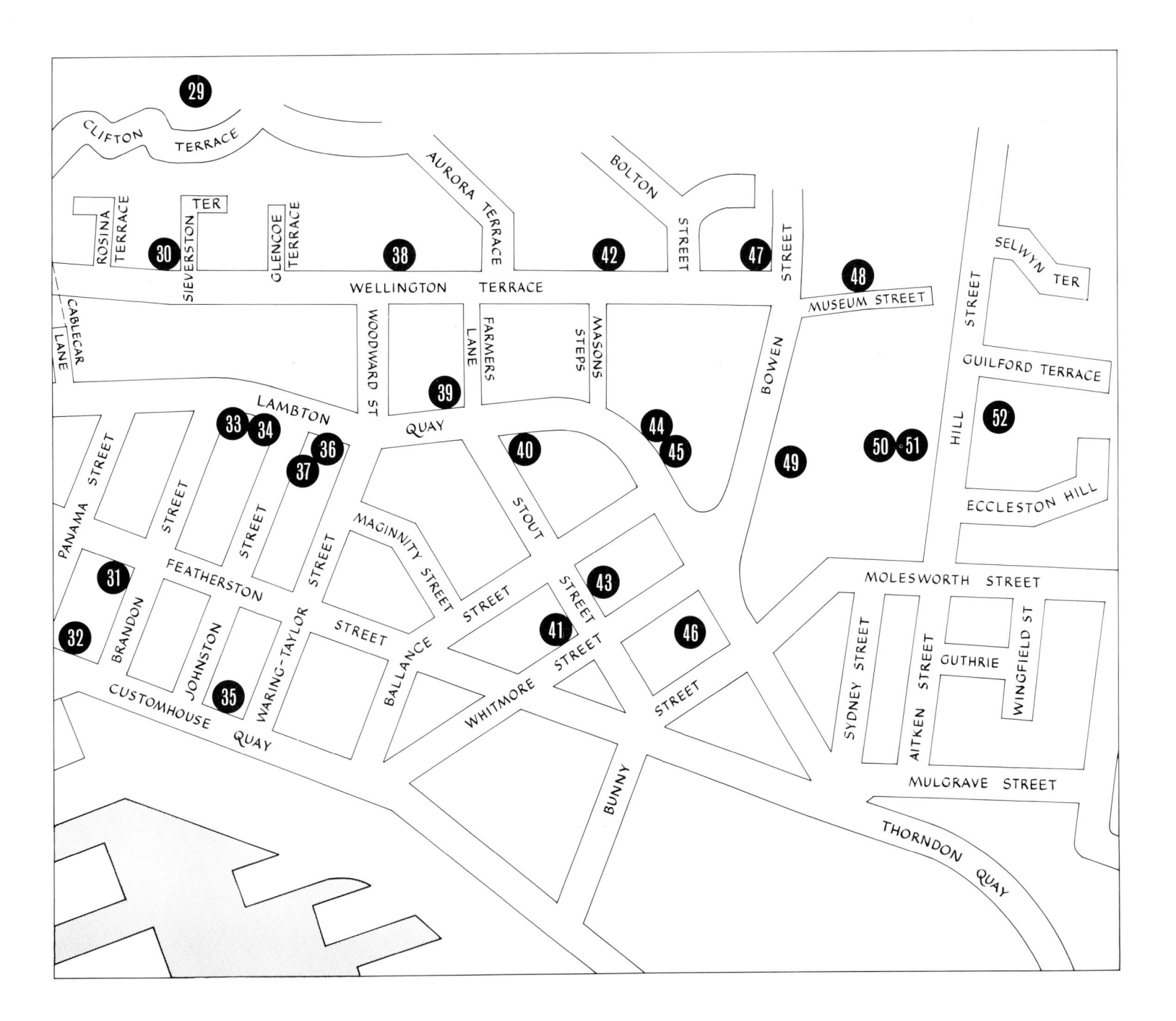

INDEX

Abel Smith Street 29
Abraham, Charles 104
Academy of Art 94
Adelaide Road 35, 138
Aitken, G. W. 150
Albert Hotel 72, 103
Albion Hotel 159
Alfred, Prince 18, 33
Allan's Pharmacy 136
Alpha Street 13, 44
AMP 64, 75, 79
Anderson, Edward 41
Anglican cathedral 20
Anti-Asiatic League 32
ANZ Bank 14, 79
Armour Avenue 39
Aro Street 130
Atack, W. H. 150
Athenaeum, 29, 30, 87, 105, 124, 125
Aubert, Mother Suzanne 27, 115
Aurora Terrace 52
Austin Street 150
Australian Widows' Fund 81

Baker's Building 64
Ballance Street 134
Bank of Australasia 75
Bankruptcy 11, 16
Bannatyne, William 41, 64

Barraud, Charles 54, 114
Barraud's Building 10
Barry and McDowell 19
Basin Reserve 128, 150, 167
Batkin E. C. 61
Beauchamp, Harold 158
Beck and Tonks 56
Beehive 18
'Bellevue' 31, 128
Benevolent Trustees 45, 47
Bethune and Hunter 16
Bethune's 11
Bing, Harris 13, 67
Bird, Blow and Wills' Circus 33
Blackett, John 141, 172
Blundell, Henry 41
Blundell, John 132
BNSW 75, 109, 165
BNZ 14, 15, 59, 62, 75, 81
Boer War 34, 171
Botanic Gardens 31, 109, 111, 127
Boulcott Street 14, 22, 72, 103, 121, 162
Bowden, Thomas 29
Bowen Street 54, 108, 136
BP House 64
Brandon Street 94, 146
Brighting, Elizabeth 159
Briscoe, Macneill 13
Britomart Street 27

Brittain, Henry 114
Brooklyn 40
Brothels 45, 46, 148, 159
Brougham Avenue 39
Brougham Bank 150
Brougham Street 150
Brown, Samuel 142
Bryant and May 13, 39
Buckle Street 20, 27, 28, 45, 115, 119
Buller, Walter 109
Burne, Joseph 54
Burnell Avenue 39
Burrows, Pierre 19, 22, 24

Cable car 141
Cable Car Lane 61
Cable, William 70
Caledonian Society 128
Cambridge Road 44
Cambridge Terrace 44, 128, 150, 169
Campbell, John 19, 96, 116, 167
Carlton Hotel 101
Carmichael and Son 75
Cars 42
Carter, Charles 22, 109
Catholic cathedral 20
Cemetery 36, 37, 144
Central Club 123
Chamber of Commerce 14
Chapple, Dr William 155

Charlesworth, Joshua   32, 39, 64, 94, 130, 132. 134, 160,
Chatfield, William   12, 13, 33, 61, 62, 67, 69, 81, 125, 128, 130, 171
Chinese   46, 47, 160
City Council   9, 15, 16, 18, 24, 26, 30, 32, 35, 36, 37, 44, 53, 70, 76, 87, 94, 116, 121, 124, 130, 136, 141, 142, 146, 150, 152, 160
City destructor   27
City Engineer   31, 125, 146
City Rifles   22
Civil Service Club   134
Claremont Grove   39, 150
Clayton, William   17, 18, 22, 31, 67, 89, 91, 126
Clere, Edmund   79
Clere, FitzGerald and Richmond   19, 22, 79, 94, 141, 165, 171
Clifton Terrace   116
Club Hotel   100
Clyde Quay   146
Clyde Quay School   28
CML   22
Coleridge, E. W. G.   160
Colonial Architect   17, 19, 67, 110
Colonial Bank   105, 124, 165
Colonial Insurance   123
Colonial Treasurer   44
Commercial Bank   124
Commercial depression   11, 12, 28, 43, 44, 45
Commercial Hotel   103, 165
Commercial Travellers Club   32, 134
Congregational Church   108
Contagious Diseases Act   46
Convalescent Home   47

Cornwall and York, Duke and Duchess of   32, 33, 116
Coromandel Street   27
Coulls, Sommerville and Wilkie   57
Courtenay Place   12, 45, 49, 142
Crichton and McKay   12, 30, 76, 125, 134, 157
Cricket Association   128
Cridland, Henry   107
Cuba Street   12, 21, 32, 36, 48, 49, 68, 139, 148, 162
Customhouse Quay   12, 14, 18, 19, 35, 64, 75, 81, 145

Dawson, William   70, 150
Days Bays Pavilion   130
Death duty   43
De Castro, C. D.   28
Diver, Dr   100
Dixon, Edward   148
Dixon Street   44, 46, 59, 155
Donald's Gardens   31
Drainage   26, 35
Drury, Alfred   169
Duco and *Duchess*   130
Duncan, Ian   42
Duncan, R. J.   62, 87

Early Closing Movement   32, 68
Earthquakes   7, 25, 83, 113, 125, 128, 147
Edmondson and Sellars   79
Egmont Street   44
Electricity   36
Ellice Avenue   39
Empire Hotel   33, 67, 73
England   48

English High School   29
Epidemics and diseases   26, 27, 44, 48, 81
Exchange   30

Featherston Street   12, 14, 18, 32, 64, 70, 73, 79, 94, 142, 145
Fever Hospital   27
Field, William   165
Fielder's   75
Fires   10, 11, 14, 17, 19, 21, 22, 62, 64, 73, 76, 79, 89, 98, 101, 105, 106, 128, 130, 154, 165, 167
Fire station   113, 132, 146
FitzGerald J. E.   150
FitzGerald's Point   39
Fitzherbert Terrace   42, 43, 116, 148, 155
Fraser's Lane   46, 159

Gamble and Creed   61
Gas   36, 142
Gaulter's Building   94
Gear, James   41, 67, 68
Gear Meat   11, 13, 69, 154
General Assembly Library   17, 88, 90, 167
George, J. R.   128
Ghuznee Street   46, 107, 147
Gibbons Building   13
Gibson, William   64
Gilmer, Hamilton   152
Gilmer, Samuel   41
Girls' High School   29, 120, 156
Glencoe Avenue   108
Godber, James   162
Goring Street   42

Government Architect 19, 24, 30, 116
Government Buildings 18, 92
Government House 17, 18, 27, 28, 54, 91, 160, 167, 169
Government Life Insurance 18, 19, 92, 94
Government Printing Office 36
Government Relieving Officer 44
Grace, Charles 28
Grace, Morgan 36, 39
Grand Arcade 103
Grand Hotel 103
Grant, J. G. 28
Grass Street 150
Gresham Hotel 128
Grey Street 49, 64, 76, 79, 165
Grosholz, M. A. E. 107
Guardian Trust 124

Haining Street 47, 160
Hales, William 111, 150
Hall, Archibald 36
Hallenstein's 11
Hamerton, R. C. 150
Hamilton, Nellie 159
Hannah, Robert 11, 41
Hannah's 39
Harbour Board 45, 84
Harbour Street 171
Harcourt, J. B. 39
Harcourt's 11, 57
Harding, Dr 56
Hawker Street 150
Hawkestone Crescent 39
Hayman Building 67
Hector, James 126

Herbert Street 114
Higginson, Henry 136
Hill, Mrs 54
Hill Street 106, 121, 144
Hobson Crescent 39
Hobson Street 39, 42, 43, 136, 148
Hobson Street bridge 136
Home for the Aged Needy 47, 160
Home for Friendless Women 47
Home for Unmarried Mothers 48
Home of Compassion 27, 115
Horowhenua 40
Hospital 25, 27, 39, 49, 113, 120
House of Representatives 17, 167
Hunter Building 123
Hunter Street 15, 79, 134, 145
Hutt Valley 36, 128, 154

Inconstant 15, 83, 103
Inspector of Nuisances 144
Island Bay 27, 115

Jacob Joseph Building 13, 57
Jervois Quay 12, 82
John Street 46, 159
Johnston and Co. 62
Johnston, Emily 42, 43, 155
Johnston, John 41, 42, 155
Johnston Street 100
Johnston, Walter 42, 43
Joseph, Jacob 10, 41, 43, 156

Kaiapoi Building 13
Kaiwharawhara 16
Karori 27, 34, 37, 39, 40, 127, 144
Katherine Avenue 155
Kelburn 40, 141

Kelburn Kiosk 141
Kelburn Parade 24, 123
Kempthorne Prosser 57
Kennedy, Martin 41, 106
Kent Terrace 128, 150, 169
King's Chambers 12, 62
Kingsdown House Academy 28
Kinnoul 60
Kirkcaldie and Stains 11, 59, 60, 100
Kirkcaldie, John 11, 41, 60, 156
Kumutoto Stream 133

Lambton Quay 9, 10, 11, 13, 14, 15, 16, 19, 21, 22, 29, 30, 33, 34, 35, 49, 52, 53, 54, 60, 61, 62, 64, 67, 68, 69, 73, 75, 76, 79, 87, 92, 96, 100, 103, 105, 108, 109, 110, 113, 123, 124, 128, 133, 136, 141, 142, 165, 169, 172
Larnach, Hon. William 24
Legislative Chamber 17
Levin and Co. 42
Levin Home for Friendless Children 47
Levin, Robert 42, 156
Levin, William 30, 39, 43, 133
Levy, Lipman 52
Levy Street 52
Lipman Street 52
Little George Street 158
Little Taranaki Street 44
Logan, Houston 54
Lorne Street 44
Ludlam, Alfred 128
Ludlam Park 128
Luke's Lane 70
Lunatic Asylum 27, 28, 47, 116, 118

Lyon and Blair 125

Macarthy, Thomas 41
Macdonald Crescent 21
Macdonald, T. K. 30, 62
Macdonald's Building 10, 62
Macky Logan Steen 12
Mair, John 94
Majoribanks Street 150
Malcolm, Miss 162
Mandel, Joseph 67, 158
Manners Street 12, 48, 56, 70, 114, 139, 142, 146
Manners Street Methodist Church 21
Mansfield, Katherine 158
Marist Brothers' School 28, 121
Martin Fountain 73
Martin, John 33, 41, 64, 73, 91
Mason and Ross 14, 75
McGrath, Peter 16
McGuire, Allan 123
McHugh, Philomene 159
McNab, James 128
McNab's Gardens 128
Melbourne Hotel 21, 101
Meyer J. H. 141
Midland Hotel 100
Midland Park 100
Mills, Edward 41, 52, 64, 70, 145
Mills's Warehouse 73
Mission to Seamen 134
'Moana Lua' 42, 156
Molesworth Street 36, 39, 104, 148, 159
Monowai 30
Morgue 20
Mormons 21

Mount Cook 31
Mount Cook Barracks 24
Mount Street 36
Mount Victoria 10, 31, 35, 38, 39, 44, 52, 118, 130, 150
Mount View 27, 28
Mulgrave Street 148
Murphy Street 18
Museum 30, 31, 126, 169
Museum Street 30, 126

Nathan, Joseph 41, 64
National Art Gallery 111
National Bank 48, 76
National Dairy Association 169
National Mutual Building 81
Naval Brigade 22, 171
Nelson, HMS 10
Newtown 18, 25, 39, 40, 49, 113, 139, 152
Newtown School 28
New Zealand Artillery 22
New Zealand Company 7
New Zealand Electrical Syndicate 132
New Zealand Insurance 79
New Zealand Society 30
New Zealand Times and *Mail* 61
'Noah's Ark' 15, 75, 81, 83, 103
Nurses' Home 27

Occidental Hotel 100
O'Connor, Maurice 141
Oddfellows Hall 29, 33, 123
O'Dea, James 103, 115, 152
Old Identities Hotel 72, 103
O'Neill, Charles 36, 106, 150

Onslow, Lord 26
Oriental Parade and Bay 16, 31, 33, 38, 39, 49, 87, 142, 147, 150
Orr's City Buffet Hotel 21, 128
Owen Street 162
Owhiro Bay 35
Oxford Hotel 100

Palace Hotel 101
Panama Street 10, 12, 62, 84
Parliament 17, 24, 30, 88, 89, 167
Parnell, Samuel 13
Pauline Home 162
Penty and Blake 12, 30, 64, 79, 123, 130, 169
Perrett's Corner 56
Petone 7, 13, 33, 154
Petre, Francis 22, 106
Phoenix Centre 61
Phoenix Insurance 81
Pilmer, A. A. G. 31
Pipitea Street 25
Pipitea Point 141
Pirie Street 150
Plimmer, John 15, 72, 83, 103
Plimmer Steps 103
Polhill Gully 16, 26
Police Station 109, 110
Poor 43, 44, 45, 46, 47, 48
Population 7, 38, 46, 147, 152, 154
Porritt Avenue 39
Portland Crescent 39
Post Office 19, 34, 64, 84, 96, 98
Prison 23, 24, 111
Private Streets 44, 49
Provincial Government 15, 17, 18, 25, 27, 28, 84, 88, 92, 94

Prudential Building 124
Public Library 30, 125
Public Trust 18, 19, 96, 134, 172
Public Works Department 17, 90

Queen Margaret College 42, 148
Queen's Bond 84
Queen's Statue 169
Queen's Wharf 15, 34, 84, 169
Queen Victoria Diamond Jubilee 27, 169
Quin Street 46

Railway Workshop 154
Railway Station 44
Railways 36, 141
Rawson, Henry 157
Reclaimed land 9, 10, 11, 15, 16, 18, 29, 32, 33, 34, 35, 54, 59, 62, 64, 81, 82, 87, 130
Reichardt's Building 60
Rhodes, Sarah 41, 113
Rhodes, W. B. 43
Richmond, Justice 150
Riddiford, E. J. 43
Riddiford, Norah 42
Rintoul Street School 28
Roading 34, 53, 136, 138
Roseneath 38, 150
Rouse and Hurrell 13
Royal Oak Hotel 21
Royal Society 30
RSA 134
Rubbish 34, 35, 82

Salvation Army 45
Salvation Army Maternity Home 48, 162
Salvation Army Rescue Home 47, 162
Salvation Army Workingmen's Hotel 45
Sargood, Son and Ewen 13
Saunders and O'Malley 15
Saunders, Joseph 158
Saunders' Lane 158
Sayes Court 52
Schwartz, George 67, 101, 146
Scotch Church 105
Scoullar and Archibald 120
Scoullar and Chisholm Building 69
Seagar, Edward 70
Seagar's Foundry 42
Shannon, George 41
Shearman, R. C. 150
Shop Hours Bill 68
Single, George 17, 88
Sloan, James 150
Slums 26, 44, 48
Smith, Benjamin 64
Smith, James 11, 41, 59
Society for the Preservation of Scenery 32
Somes Island 48
Soup Kitchen 45
South British Insurance 124
SPCA 70
Spiritualists 21
St Andrew's, Lambton Quay 105
St Andrew's, the Terrace 21, 22, 105, 165
St George Hotel 72, 103
St James's, Lower Hutt 154
St John's Ambulance 113

St John's, Willis Street 21, 22
St Joseph's, Buckle Street 27
St Joseph's Home for Incurables 27, 48
St Joseph's Industrial School 28, 47, 106
St Mark's, Basin Reserve 21, 128
St Mary's, Boulcott Street 22
St Mary's, Hill Street 21, 22, 106
St Mary's School 28, 106, 121
St Paul's, Mulgrave Street 21, 104
St Paul's School 28
St Peter's School 28
St Peter's, Willis Street 21, 22, 106
Stains, Robert 11, 156
Star Boating Club 32, 61, 171
Star Chambers 61
Stout Street 22, 96, 110, 134, 145, 172
Street lighting 36, 142
Sturdee Street 46
Suicide 45
Supreme Court 22, 109, 110
Swan, John 42, 61, 76, 141, 156
Sydney Street 17
Synagogue 21, 108

T and G Building 123
Taranaki Street 20
Taranaki Street Boys' School 28
Te Aro 10, 39, 147, 152
Te Aro Baths 31
Te Aro Dispensary 114
Te Aro Flat 38, 39, 47, 48, 147
Te Aro foreshore 9, 35, 142
Te Aro Grammar School 28
Te Aro House 11, 48, 59

Te Hopai Home   160
Telephone exchange   145
Temple Chambers   64
Tennyson Street   44
Terrace   10, 33, 38, 49 52, 54, 57, 105, 108, 116, 119, 133, 136, 138, 157, 162, 165
Terrace School   28, 116
Terry, Lionel   160
Thatcher, Frederick   104
Theatre Royal   36, 100
Theatre Royal Hotel   100
Thompson, Shannon Building   62
Thompson Street   60, 152
Thorndon   10, 15, 31, 38, 46, 113, 120, 128, 130, 141, 148, 159
Thorndon Baths   32, 130
Thorndon Esplanade   32, 130
Thorndon School   28
Tinakori Road   42, 105, 127
Tory Street   87
Town Belt   31, 49, 116, 118
Town Hall   18, 32, 33, 94, 132, 139, 146
Toxward, Christian   10, 11, 14, 18, 25, 26, 27, 28, 54, 59, 64, 73, 75, 76, 79, 92, 100, 104, 105, 106, 108, 111, 116, 118, 119, 165
Trams   36, 38, 40, 76, 138, 139, 141
Treasury   18
Tringham, Charles   31, 54, 56, 62, 101, 128
Trocadero Hotel   165
Turnbull, Thomas   10, 11, 13, 14, 17, 18, 19, 21, 22, 29, 30, 32, 42, 56, 59, 60, 64, 67, 75, 76, 79, 81, 94, 98, 100, 120, 121, 123, 124, 125, 133, 154, 155, 156
Turnbull, Walter   41, 43
Turnbull, W. and G. Building   13, 64
Turnbull, William   12, 40, 60, 76, 81, 117
Turner, Charles   157

Unemployment   43, 44, 110
Union Bank   14, 72, 73, 103, 165
University   24, 123
Upland Farm   141

Van Staveren, Herman   47, 108
Veitch and Allan Building   12
Veitch, Alexander   150
Veterans' Home, Auckland   160
Victoria Building   33
Victoria Hospital for Chronic Diseases   27, 33
Victoria Street   12, 13, 42, 67, 114, 134

Wadestown   16
Wairarapa   38, 40, 67, 72, 154
Wairarapa Farmers Co-op   57
Waiwera   34
Ward, Thomas   53
Waring-Taylor, Misses   11
Waterfront   15, 84
Waterloo House   59
Watermen   84
Water supply   11, 26
Wealthy   41, 42, 43
Webster, Dr Garcia   157
Wellesley Block   40
Wellington Academical Institution   28
Wellington Academy   28
Wellington Bowling Club   130
Wellington Club   32, 33, 57, 133, 136
Wellington College   29, 116, 118, 128
Wellington Education Board   119
Wellington Ferry Co.   130
Wellington Industrial Exhibition   172
Wellington-Manawatu Railway   28, 36
Wellington-Masterton Railway   36
Wellington Woollen Co.   154
Western Hotel   103
Westpac Tower   76
Wheeler Rev.   28
Whitcombe and Tombs   76
Wilkinson, Catherine   150
Wilkinson, David   150
Wilkinson's Gardens   31, 38
Willeston Street   12, 171
Williams, J. H.   130
Williams, Mary Anne   134
Williams, T. C.   42, 43, 148
Williams, William   134
Willis Street   10, 11, 12, 14, 21, 34, 53, 56, 67, 72, 101, 103, 107, 147, 155, 162
Willis Street School   28
Wilson, J. and A.   96
Winder, George   48
Windhover   150
Wingfield Street   159
Wirth Brothers Circus   30
Woodward Street   108, 136, 157
Wordsworth Street   130
Wright Street   26

Ziman, David   39